The Challenges of Democratic Consolidation in Portugal

The Challenges of Democratic Consolidation in Portugal

Political, Economic, and Military Issues, 1976–1991

PAUL CHRISTOPHER MANUEL

PRAEGER

Westport, Connecticut
London

Library of Congress Cataloging-in-Publication Data

Manuel, Paul Christopher.
The challenges of democratic consolidation in Portugal : political, economic, and military issues, 1976–1991 / Paul Christopher Manuel.
p. cm.
Includes bibliographical references and index.
ISBN 0-275-94849-8 (alk. paper)
1. Portugal—Politics and government—1974– 2. Portugal—Economic conditions—1974– 3. Civil-military relations—Portugal. 4. Democracy—Portugal. I. Title.
JN8502 1996a
320.9469'09'045—dc20 95-43762

British Library Cataloguing in Publication Data is available.

Library of Congress Catalog Card Number: 95-43762
ISBN: 0-275-94849-8

First published in 1996

Praeger Publishers, 88 Post Road West, Westport, CT 06881
An imprint of Greenwood Publishing Group, Inc.

Printed in the United States of America

The paper used in this book complies with the Permanent Paper Standard issued by the National Information Standards Organization (Z39.48–1984).

10 9 8 7 6 5 4 3 2 1

para Xartinho, Mata do Rei, e a família

Contents

Tables

Preface

I first traveled to Portugal in 1976 to visit my family, and have returned almost every year since. These voyages have, by chance, coincided with the rapid political and economic transformations accompanying the inauguration of the country's new democratic regime. In my experience, the most striking evidence of these changes is in my grandparents' twin villages of Xartinho and Mata do Rei. These villages are situated in the Santarém district, close to the border of the district of Leira, in central Portugal. When my grandfather showed me around in 1978 and 1979, the village's sole telephone and television were located in the café, there were no schools, the road was unpaved, and electrical and sanitary conditions were minimal. These impoverished conditions were but a small legacy of the forty-eight years of authoritarian rule, which had successfully endeavored, for the most part, to keep the countryside rural, agricultural, and undeveloped. The people had learned to expect nothing from the regime in Lisbon, and the only viable way to escape the poverty was to emigrate to, among other places, France, Germany, Brazil, Canada, or the United States.

Since 1976 the years of democratic rule by, arguably, a Lisbon-based political elite, have brought some infrastructure improvements to Xartinho and Mata do Rei, including a paved road and the opening of a school. In spite of these improvements, many village people still complain that it is difficult to get the attention of local governmental officials because their tiny villages are situated at the edge of the Santarém administrative district.

I spent the 1990-1991 academic year researching my doctoral thesis at the University of Coimbra, and was surprised to see a nationally televised news report the night of 13 January 1991 stating that the inhabitants of Xartinho and Mata do Rei had boycotted that day's presidential election. Feeling outnumbered and ignored, the village people finally took the drastic act of not voting to gain the attention of their elected representatives. This electoral boycott was not over abstract principles of democratic theory, but involved frustrated expectations: the village people expected that their democratic government should do something about their problems, and were frustrated with the slow pace of change.

This example relates to a larger theme of comparative interest in the Portuguese case of democratic consolidation, which is how political and economic variables interact. The causal relationship among these factors is a complex issue, but it is clear that political stability and economic recovery can facilitate the process of democratic consolidation. José María Maravall has usefully conceptualized this fundamental relationship, observing that "once democracies are reestablished after a period of dictatorial rule, new problems emerge. The efficiency of the new political system, and not just its legitimacy, becomes the main issue—that is, the capacity of democracy to solve problems and fulfill expectations."[1] This book is interested in how, by solving problems and fulfilling expectations, the new democratic regime in Portugal has improved its chances for long-term durability.

This study divides the consolidation period into three recognizable phases, during which the new regime has had to confront political, economic and military challenges. Chapter 1 introduces and examines the players and challenges of the transition. Chapter 2 analyses the first period, characterized by the weakness of the National Assembly, governmental instability and persistent economic problems. Chapter 3 studies the second period, noting how the newly emergent Democratic Alliance political movement empowered the National Assembly to confront the military challenge. Chapter 4 delineates the third period, marked by continued governmental stability and economic recovery. By 1991, the largely successful resolution of these challenges had improved the regime's prospects for survival. Chapter 5 summarizes and concludes the study.

NOTE

1. José María Maravall, "Politics and Policy: Economic Reforms in Southern Europe," in Luis Carlos Bresser Pereira, José María Maravall and Adam Przeworski, eds., *Economic Reforms in New Democracies: A Social Democratic Approach* (Cambridge: Cambridge University Press, 1993), 77.

Acknowledgments

I would like to express my appreciation to Nancy Bermeo, Thomas Bruneau, Carlos Gaspar, Walter Opello, António Costa Pinto, Boaventura de Sousa Santos and António Vitorino for their support and encouragement of my research on Portugal. I presented draft versions of this project at a conference organized by the Department of Portuguese and Brazilian Studies at Brown University in the fall of 1994, and to the Iberian Studies Group at the Center of European Studies at Harvard University in the spring of 1996. I would like to thank all of the participants at these meetings for their comments, especially Dietrich Rueschemeyer, João Espada and Onésimo Almeida. I am grateful to my doctoral mentor at Georgetown University, Eusébio Mujal-León, and the members of my dissertation committee, Arturo Valenzuela and Robert Lieber, for the continuing benefit of their insight. The Fulbright Commission, the Association for the Support of Portuguese Descendants, and the National Endowment for the Humanities have provided financial support.

I gratefully acknowledge the contributions to my thinking by Valerie Bunce of Cornell University's Department of Government, who challenged me to refine my notions regarding democratic consolidation during her NEH seminar on European democratization in the summer of 1995. José Alvarez-Junco and Joaquín Fernández-Castro of the Tufts-Harvard Iberian Studies group have organized valuable seminars on the issues of political change in Portugal and Spain over the past few years at Harvard's Center for European Studies. Five students at Saint Anselm College helped with the research for this book: Kara Welch, Michael Guilfoyle, Sean Tanguay, Steven Wall and Matt Sullivan.

I thank all the members of my family in the United States and in Portugal for their help. In particular, Joaquim and Barbara Manuel, Guido and Mary Ida Cammisa, Joaquim and Maria Manuel, Louis and Elvira Lagomarsino, Maryann Lagomarsino, Joaquim and Hilda Manuel, Mark and Rosemary Manuel, David

Manuel, Jim Cammisa, Michael Cammisa, José Narciso, Mariazinha Martins Narciso, José Costa, Joaquim Costa, Teresa Martins Costa, José Ferreira, Sara Ferreira, Carolina Ferreira and Ana Maria Martins Narciso have all played a major role in my life and work. Most important, I would like to thank my wife, Anne Marie, for all of the patience and support she gave me during the research and writing of this book as she was engaged in the research and writing of her own book, *Governments as Interest Groups: Intergovernmental Lobbying and the Federal System* (Westport, CT: Praeger, 1995). *To Anne Marie: obrigado, beijos, saudades e amor.* Although many have helped, the virtues and failures of this book are mine alone.

Abbreviations

AD—Democratic Alliance (Aliança Democrática)
APU—United People's Alliance (Acção Nacional Popular)
AR—National Assembly (Assembleia da República)
ASD—Democratic Social Action (Acção Democrática Social)
CDS—Social Democratic Center Party (Partido do Centro Democrático Social)
CDU—Democratic Unitary Coalition (Coligação Democrático Unitário)
CGTP—General Confederation of Portuguese Workers (Confederação Geral dos Trabalhadores Portugueses)
CR—Council of the Revolution (Conselho da Revolução)
CUF—United Manufacturing Company (Companhia União Fabril)
DGS—Directorate General of Security (Direcção-Geral da Segurança)
EEC—European Economic Community
FP-25—Popular Forces of 25 April (Forças Populares de 25 Abril)
FRS—Republican and Socialist Front (Frente Republicana e Socialista)
FSP—Popular Socialist Front (Frente Socialista Popular)
FUP—Popular Unity Force (Força Popular Unido)
IMF—International Monetary Fund
MDP—Portuguese Democratic Movement (Movimento Democrático Português)
MES—Movement of the Socialist Left (Movimento da Esquerda Socialista)
MFA—Armed Forces Movement (Movimento das Forças Armadas)
NATO—North Atlantic Treaty Organization
PCP—Portuguese Communist Party (Partido Comunista Português)
PIDE—International Police for the Defense of the State (Policia Internacional da Defesa do Estado)
PNS—National Solidarity Party (Partido Nacional de Solidariedade)
PPD—Popular Democratic Party (Partido Popular Democrático)
PPM—Popular Monarchist Party (Partido Popular Monárquico)

PRD—Democratic Renewal Party (Partido Renovador Democrático)
PS—Socialist Party (Partido Socialista)
PSD—Social Democrat Party (Partido Social Democrata)
UDP—Popular Democratic Union (União Democrática Popular)
UEDS—Union of the Democratic and Socialist Left (União da Esquerda Democrática e Socialista)
UGT—General Union of Workers (União Geral dos Trabalhadores)

The Challenges of Democratic Consolidation in Portugal

1

The Challenges and the Players of the Portuguese Democratic Consolidation

After a tortuous two-year transition period, Portugal inaugurated its new democratic regime on 23 July 1976. The transition period, initiated by the successful 25 April 1974 Armed Forces Movement (MFA) coup d'état against the authoritarian *Estado Novo* regime, had brought about a prolonged national debate regarding the new form of government and social organization the country would adopt. After six provisional governments, three elections, and two failed coup attempts, the country finally opted for the creation of a West European-style democracy. Hoping that the worst was over, the Portuguese people anxiously awaited the arrival of stable and prosperous times.[1]

Although the democratic Constitution of 1976 had ended the political and military intrigue of the two-year transition period, the actual consolidation of the new Portuguese democratic regime was not a self-evident proposition. Over the next fifteen years, the young regime faced serious political, economic and military challenges that threatened its continued existence.[2] Drawing from the useful analytic guidelines framed by J. Samuel Valenzuela in "Democratic Consolidation in Post-Transitional Settings: Notion, Process, and Facilitating Conditions"[3] this chapter introduces the key issues, challenges and players of the Portuguese democratic consolidation.

THE PORTUGUESE CASE OF DEMOCRATIC CONSOLIDATION

Theoretical Issues

Sometimes lumped together, the issues of democratic transition and democratic consolidation are both conceptually and empirically distinct. Whereas transitologists seek to discover the origins of a democratic regime, consolidologists search for the variables that keep a regime robust, stable and durable. Transitologists, inspired by Machiavelli and rejecting the post-1945 theoretical effort to identify the developmental, class or cultural prerequisites for the establishment of democracy, have argued that the "zone of transition" (defined as the period of authoritarian regime collapse, authority void, and the eventual creation and installation of a new democratic regime) is controlled by political factors.[4] Conceptualizing the transition period as a chaotic, heady time, transitologists emphasize a probabilistic model of political change in which the choices, strategies, calculations and miscalculations of the relevant actors determine a transition's political outcome.[5]

Dankwart Rustow's 1970 article entitled "Transitions to Democracy" helped launch the transitologist theoretical movement. In that analysis of moments of democratic political change, Rustow set out four necessary conditions for a successful transition to democracy: national unity as a background condition, a prolonged and unresolved elite power struggle, a decision by the key political elite to open the political process to civil society, and the habituation by civil and elite sectors to democratic practices.[6] Although others have since refined and enhanced Rustow's notion, it remains as one of the centerpieces of transitologist literature.[7] Ironically, Rustow's final transition phase, "the habituation to democratic procedures,"[8] signals a conceptual shift to the consolidation phase. He describes politics in the habituation phase as "above all, a process for resolving conflicts within human groups—whether these arise from the clash of interests or from uncertainty about the future. . . . With its basic practice of multilateral debate, democracy in particular involves a process of trial and error, a joint learning experience."[9] Rustow's observations, especially "resolving conflict," "multilateral debate," and "democracy as a process of trial and error" bring us to the notion of democratic consolidation.

During a transition, time is at a premium, and a political actor typically cannot afford to make many errors. If a political actor were even to attempt to learn by trial and error during a transitional moment, he would likely be outmaneuvered by his opponents.[10] Conversely, the consolidation of a democratic regime obliges political actors to learn the skills of multilateral debate and to develop peaceful mechanisms to resolve conflict. Distinguishing between transitologists and consolidologists, Terry Lynn Karl and Philippe Schmitter have astutely noted that whereas Machiavelli serves as the theoretical patron saint of transitologists, consolidologists, following Plato and Aristotle, seek "to explain why . . . stable patterns of authority and privilege manage to survive."[11] In that search, consolidologists ask, among other questions, whether the new civilian democratic regime has subordinated the military to its authority, if the former authoritarian regime elites have accepted the new democratic regime, and to what degree the new regime is successfully managing political and social conflict.[12] Thus, Rustow's observations at the end of his article stop at the conceptual point where this study begins—with the consolidation of a democratic regime.

The Challenges of the Portuguese Case

In the Portuguese case, inasmuch as the "transititions to democracy" scholarship had accurately conceptualized the emergence of the democratic regime as primarily a political process, the consolidation of that regime involved a much more complex mix of variables.[13] That is, before the new democratic regime could become consolidated, it had to deal successfully with its political, economic and military challenges. Failing to do so, the regime would face almost certain breakdown.

The Political Challenge

The political challenge required that the new regime achieve governmental stability in Lisbon and develop linkage organizations in civil society.[14] In both of these areas, political parties took center stage.

The Constitution of 1976: Seeking Governmental Stability. During the Constituent Assembly's constitutional deliberations in the summer of 1975 and spring of 1976, delegates were concerned with essentially three dimensions of governmental stability. First, they aspired to craft a regime that was neither excessively unstable nor fraught with party divisions.[15] Second, they sought to secure a dominant place for political parties in the new regime. Finally, they wanted to create a moderating executive institution which would protect the regime against excessive parliamentarism.[16] The result of their deliberations was a presidential-parliamentarian hybrid. Loosely borrowing from the French dual-executive model, the Constitution provides for both a President and a Prime Minister.

The President was granted independent authority and legitimacy outside of the National Assembly. Whereas the law making function rests with the Prime Minister and the National Assembly, the President's role is, following Articles 136–141, to monitor activities of the government, chair the Council of the Revolution, and veto legislation. Further, in the event of a stalemate in the National Assembly, the President has the power to dismiss the Prime Minister, appoint a new Prime Minister or call for new elections. This moderating role has been very important for Portugal during the first eleven years of the new regime. Further, Articles 124 and 131 provide that the President is elected by universal suffrage to a five-year term, and Article 126 prohibits any president from serving more than two consecutive terms.[17]

The Constitution provides for the election of 250 deputies, using the d'Hondt system of proportional representation. That system, which allocates seats based on the highest average vote obtained, has led to governmental stability and reduced the number of political parties in Portugal.[18] Thomas Bruneau has observed that since the introduction of the d'Hondt system in 1976, the larger parties have been overrepresented in the National Assembly in relation to the votes cast for them, the mid-sized parties have been allocated seats roughly in relation to the votes they have received, and the smaller parties have disappeared for the most part. In the constitutional period, only one small party, the Popular Democratic Union (UDP), representing a far-left intellectual Lisbon constituency, has managed to win a seat.[19] The d'Hondt system has aided the goal of governmental stability both by limiting the number of parties in the system and by providing incentives for the larger parties to cooperate, leading to a number of electoral coalitions in the Portuguese elections since 1976.

The Constitution of 1976 also carves out a special place for the political parties. It specifies that only officially recognized political parties can present candidates for Parliament, and requires that any amendment to the Constitution be passed by a two-thirds majority of the party-controlled National Assembly.[20] Members of the National Assembly must stand for reelection at least every four years.[21]

The Key Players: Political Parties. Although the Constitution provides a large role for the political parties, the substantial ideological and personal conflicts among and within them has threatened governmental stability and the consolidation of the new regime. Since 1976, there have been five significant political parties in Portugal, most of which have experienced divisive internal battles.

The Social Democrat Party (PSD) has been the political party most responsible for the return of governmental stability in the 1976 to 1991 period. Originally called the Popular Democratic Party (PPD), it was founded in May 1974 by members of the regime's liberal opposition, including Francisco Sá Carneiro, Joaquim Magalhães Mota and Francisco Pinto Balsemão. It represents a center and center-right constituency, and is supported by moderate voters. It has fared very well in the traditionalist and religious constituencies in the northern regions, the islands and the city of Oporto. The PSD has suffered one notable internal division since the initiation of the democratic regime. In 1979, party leader Francisco Sá Carneiro alienated thirty-seven of the party's representatives when he arbitrarily decided to withdraw the party's support for the administration of Carlos Mota Pinto. Led by António Sousa Franco and António Rebelo de Sousa, those thirty-seven members resigned from the PSD and formed a new party, the Independent Social Democrats. Undaunted, Sá Carneiro organized an alliance of center-right parties called the Democratic Alliance, and secured a majority in the 1979 and 1980 legislative elections. In the 1987 and 1991 legislative elections the PSD, led by Aníbal Cavaco Silva, won absolute majorities, and has since been a central force in the regime's consolidation.[22]

The Socialist Party (PS) has been a key player since 1974. Although there has been a strong socialist tradition in Portugal since the end of the nineteenth century, the current Socialist Party was organized by Mário Soares and other exiled Socialists living in Bonn, Germany, in 1973. The PS represents a moderate, leftist electorate, and is committed to both socialism and democracy. It has received the bulk of its support from the city of Lisbon, the center regions of the country, and from the Algarve region. Its vague ideological identity has led to several party divisions since 1976. Among these, three have been significant. In 1978, António Lopes Cardoso resigned from the PS, and formed a far-left party called the Democratic and Socialist Left (UEDS). In 1979, a group of moderate Socialists, including António Barreto and José Medeiros Ferreira, joined the center-right Democratic Alliance. In the mid-1980s, the "histórico" movement within the PS accused Mário Soares and other party leaders of having lost touch with the party's history and Marxist ideology. Soares defeated the "históricos" with the help of a group known as the "new Socialists." Led by António Guterres and Vítor Constâncio, these "new Socialists" are committed to efficiency and pragmatic policies, and removed all references to Marxism from the party platform in 1986.[23]

The Portuguese Communist Party (PCP), founded in 1921, has played an important role in the consolidation by providing a vehicle for disenchanted leftists to participate in the system. It advocates Stalinist policies and enjoys its largest base of support from the largely landless workers in the southern Alentejo region, and from workers in the Lisbon-Setúbal industrial belt. Beginning in the 1940s, the party's secretary-general, Álvaro Cunhal, established a disciplined, clandestine network of party cells throughout the country. The PCP was the only opposition party to survive in Portugal during the Salazar/Caetano dictatorship. Since the establishment of democracy, the Communist party has been the most vociferous defender of the socialist gains of 25 April 1974, and has steadfastly resisted the move to capitalist policies. To improve its electoral chances, the PCP has frequently formed coalitions with smaller parties, including Francisco Pereira de Moura's Portuguese Democratic Movement (MDP) and the Greens.[24] The Communists have never been invited to serve in a Constitutional government, but continue to participate in the democratic regime.

In spite of its name, the Social Democratic Center Party (CDS) represents some of the most conservative elements of Portuguese society. Given the leftist shift of the political equation in Portugal after the 25 April 1974 coup, no political party dared to state explicitly that it had a conservative, right-wing agenda. Understanding the dynamics of the transition's political situation, a group of conservatives, including Diogo Freitas do Amaral, Adelino Amaro da

Costa, and Xavier Pintado organized this right-wing party. The CDS espouses a traditionalist ideology and supports capitalism. Like the PSD, it appeals to voters in the city of Oporto, some central regions around the city of Leiria, the northern areas and in the islands.[25] The CDS has also proven to be a pragmatic party: in 1978, it formed a government coalition with the Socialist Party, and in 1979, it joined the Democratic Alliance electoral front with the PSD and the People's Popular Monarchist Party (PPM). Over the past few years the CDS has had to contend with a loss of support to the PSD. As with the PCP on the left, the CDS has helped in the process of democratic consolidation by linking right and far-right constituencies to the regime.

Although no longer a significant party, the Democratic Renewal Party (PRD) played a very important role in the process of democratic consolidation. The PRD was formed in 1985 as a political vehicle for President Ramalho Eanes. It proposed a poorly defined moderate leftist political program designed to "renew Portuguese democracy." Soon after it was formed, the PRD, based on the appeal of President Eanes, gained almost 18 percent of the votes in the 1985 legislative elections. For the next two years the party continued to propose a vague ideology, and did not build up a good organizational network in civil society. In the 1987 legislative elections, the PRD novelty had worn off, and the party managed only 4 percent of the vote. That poor result forced former President Eanes to resign his party leadership post, and the party has since disbanded. The rise and fall of the PRD was a good lesson for the new regime: its rapid rise demonstrated that the democratic regime was responsive to its constituency, whereas its rapid fall taught that to endure, a party must present some type of understandable ideology and, perhaps more important, develop organizational strength in civil society.

The Play of the Parliamentary Game. The difficulties of the military and economic challenges, combined with the ideological and personal differences among and within the political parties, have led to a number of governmental changes during the process of consolidation. As indicated in Table 1.1, the country suffered from political instability during the 1976–1987 period, when there were five legislative elections, leading to the formation of ten governments. Remarkably, the elections of 1987 and 1991 provided the PSD with an absolute majority in the National Assembly, increasing political stability, and helping the process of democratic consolidation. Those elections delegated to the PSD the responsibility to provide effective and purposeful leadership for the democratic regime.

Table 1.1 National Assembly Electoral Results in Portugal, 1976–1991

Date	PCP(1)	PS(2)	PSD(3)	AD	CDS	PRD(4)	Others(5)
2 Apr 76	14.35%	34.87%	24.38%	-----	16.0%	-----	5.7%
Seats won	40	107	73		42		1
2 Dec 79	18.8%	27.3%	----->	42.52%	<------	-----	5.9%
Seats won	47	74		128			1
5 Oct 80	16.75%	26.65%	----->	44.91	<------	-----	5.6%
Seats won	44	74		134			1
25 Apr 83	18.07	36.12%	27.0%	-----	12.56%	-----	3.3%
Seats won	44	101	75		30		0
6 Oct 85	15.49%	20.77%	29.87%	-----	9.69%	17.92%	4.0%
Seats won	22	57	88		22	45	0
19 Jul 87	12.14%	22.24%	50.22%	-----	4.44%	4.91%	8.8%
Seats won	31	60	148		4	7	0
6 Oct 91	8.8%	29.1%	50.43%	-----	4.4%	-----	4.9%
Seats won	17	69	130		5		1

Notes: (1) The PCP (Portuguese Communist Party or Partido Comunista Português) ran with the MDP (Portuguese Democratic Movement or Movimento Democrático Português) in 1980 and 1983 as the APU (United People's Action or Acção Nacional Popular); the PCP and the MDP ran with the Greens (os Verdes) as the CDU (Democratic Unitary Coalition, or Coligação Democrático Unitário) in 1987 and 1991. (2) The PS (Socialist Party or Partido Socialista) ran with the UEDS (Union of the Democratic and Social Left or União da Esquerda Democrática e Socialista) and the MES (Movement of the Socialist Left or Movimento da Esquerda Socialista) as the FRS (Republican and Socialist Front or Frente Republicana e Socialista) in 1983; (3) The PSD (Social Democrat Party or Partido Social Democrata) was known as the PPD (Popular Democratic Party or Partido Popular Democrático) in 1976. The PSD ran with the CDS (Party of the Social Democratic Center or Partido do Centro Democrático Social) and the PPM (Popular Monarchist Party or Partido Popular Monárquico) as the AD (Democratic Alliance or Aliança Democrática) in 1979 and 1980. (4) The PRD (Democratic Renewal Party or Partido Renovador Democrático) disbanded in 1991. (5) The far-left UDP (Popular Democratic Union or União Democrática Popular) won one seat in 1976, 1979 and 1980. The pro-pensioners PNS (National Solidarity Party or Partido Nacional de Solidariedade) won one seat in 1991. *Sources:* Manuel Braga da Cruz and Miguel Lobo Antunes, "Revolutionary Transition and the Problems of Parliamentary Institutionalization: the Case of the Portuguese National Assembly," in Ulrike Liebert and Maurizio Cotta, editors, *Parliament and Democratic Consolidation in Southern Europe* (London: Pinter 1990), 154–183; *Atlas Eleitoral: Resultados Eleitorais, 1975–1980* (Lisbon: Editorial Progresso Social e Democracia, 1981); *News of Portugal,* 7 October 1991.

Extending Stakes to Civil Society. A successful democratic consolidation also requires that the newly democratized regime reach out to civil society. In this regard, Daniel Levine accurately notes that "the whole package only works if elites and popular groups are linked in mutually valued and enduring ways. Of course, the ties are neither inevitable nor automatic. They reflect continuous organizational effort, a measure of accountability, and participation by popular sectors in ways that grant legitimacy to the leaders whose actions and stated goals resonate with their own needs."[26]

In the Portuguese case, the task of organizing civil society fell to the political parties. Political parties enjoy certain advantages over other actors, including national political visibility, strategic flexibility and tactical discretion.[27] In addition, in a democratic setting, political parties would want, arguably, to expand and deepen their base of support among the people to improve their electoral chances. The net result of this organizational process would be to connect more people to the democratic regime.[28] Thus, the consolidation, following Geoffrey Pridham, "is less exclusive to the role of elites than the transition, placing more attention on the relationship between system and society."[29]

Successful organizational efforts, as noted by Stepan, Levine, Linz and Diamond, among others, may make people less likely to participate in anti-system terrorist activities.[30] In the post-1976 period, only one significant anti-system terrorist group has been active in Portugal, the Popular Forces of 25 April (FP-25). They are a troublesome group but have not posed a major danger to the regime. The organization of civil sectors is a continuous and important element in the process of democratic regime consolidation, tilting the political incentive structure for the citizen toward participation in the regime, thus enhancing the regime's long-term survival.[31]

The Economic Challenge

The economic challenge of the consolidation period required that the elected governments promote economic recovery and social fairness. If they failed in either of these areas, the young regime risked losing support for its democratic institutions.

The 1974-1976 political transition inflicted a high economic cost. The provisional governments had made a number of costly decisions, including rapid increases in wages and public expenditures, and assumed responsibility for the short-term care of the 600,000 *retornados*, or Portuguese returning from the former African colonies. Combined, these factors led to budget deficits, drops in income derived from tourism, and decreases in remittances from emigrants.[32] Further, as Table 1.2 indicates, from 1974 to 1990, the Portuguese economy suffered from low growth rates in industry and agriculture, and experienced high rates of inflation and unemployment.

Starting in 1977, the regime turned to the International Monetary Fund (IMF) and to the European Economic Community (EEC) for financial assistance. As a prerequisite for immediate relief, the IMF forced Portugal to implement a series of very difficult austerity measures that negatively impacted large sectors of the population. The prolonged negotiations with the EEC did not provide immediate relief for the economic situation, but it has helped stabilize the economy after Portugal's entry in the EEC on 1 January 1986. In the late 1970s and early 1980s, however, the economic challenge loomed as a serious threat to regime stability.

Table 1.2 Rates of Growth, Inflation and Unemployment, 1974–1990

(% Change)

Year	GDP	Industry	Agriculture	Inflation	Unemployment
1974	2.2	3.1	2.1	26.0	5.3
1975	-4.7	-9.7	- 1.9	17.0	11.2
1976	6.0	4.5	-1.5	18.2	13.8
1977	5.6	11.0	-10.0	27.3	12.6
1978	0.31	3.3	4.0	22.0	8.4
1979	4.5	5.0	9.0	24.2	8.1
1980	4.9	6.0	2.1	16.6	7.9
1981	1.8	1.5	-10.4	20.0	8.6
1982	3.2	2.8	9.2	23.0	7.1
1983	-0.3	1.0	-5.0	25.5	7.7
1984	-1.6	-0.8	2.8	29.3	8.3
1985	3.3	4.5	5.5	19.3	8.5
1986	4.3	5.0	2.5	11.7	8.4
1987	4.7	4.2	6.5	9.4	7.0
1988	4.6	7.0	-12.0	9.7	5.7
1989	5.5	5.0	13.5	13.0	5.0
1990	4.2	4.7	----	14.4	4.7

Source: Dulce M. Soares, "Social Concertation and the Democratic Social Consensus: Theory and Praxis in the Portugal of the 1980s." Paper delivered to the Iberian Studies Group, Center for European Studies, Harvard University, 17 March 1995. Taken from B. Baer and A. P. N. Leite, "The Peripheral Economy: Its Performance in Isolation and Integration," *Luso–Brazilian Review* 29 (1992): 18.

The Military Challenge

According to the Constitution of 1976, the Council of the Revolution (CR) was granted a supreme oversight role in the new system. The military challenge required that the elected officials pass a revision of the Constitution abolishing the CR. The military has traditionally played a large role in Portuguese politics and government. During the Salazar/Caetano *Estado Novo* regime (1933–1974), the military leadership maintained de facto control of the armed forces, and there were no independent civilian review boards for military activities.[33] Salazar often consulted with military leaders, and a military officer held the position of President throughout the life of the regime.[34] In fact, the *Estado Novo* managed to last forty-eight years in no small part due to the support of the military, and was overthrown by a military intervention.[35]

The Military Modality of the Democratic Transition. In contrast to the pacted Spanish transition to democracy, the 25 April 1974 coup against the Salazar/Caetano regime by the Armed Forces Movement (MFA) represented a radical break from the previous regime. Political turmoil continued for almost two years after the coup because the MFA itself was a fragmented body. By December 1975, however, the MFA's moderate, pro-democratic faction had successfully outmaneuvered and discredited their chief opponents, including Vasco Gonçalves, who had been in favor of the construction of an East European Communist state, and Otelo Saraiva de Carvalho, who had been in favor of the creation of a radical Third World Socialist state.[36]

By cleansing both leftist and rightist anti-democratic elements from the political equation, the military modality of the Portuguese transition may be seen as a facilitator of the democratic consolidation process, in that no significant anti-democratic political party remained in Portugal after 1976.[37] However, the modality of the transition also posed a major danger for the regime's consolidation, because no political party had the organizational base to countervail military authority in 1976.[38]

Although much more moderate than the other MFA factions, the victorious MFA officers still believed that the new democratic regime should be based on the twin principles of electoral and revolutionary legitimacy. Consequently, the MFA ensured that the Constitution of 1976 granted its leadership body, the Council of the Revolution (CR), a supreme oversight role in the new regime. Articles 142–149 delegate to the CR the responsibility to ensure that the elected governments stay "faithful to the spirit of the Portuguese Revolution of 25 April 1974," whereas Articles 1, 2 and 80, among others, commit Portugal to the development of a classless society and socialism.[39] Further, to ensure that the CR had the power to enforce these provision, Article 147 grants the CR veto power over any legislation it deems unconstitutional. In these ways, the Constitution of 1976 elevated revolutionary legitimacy above electoral legitimacy.[40]

The supremacy of revolutionary legitimacy posed an interesting paradox for the young democracy: What would the military do if the people rejected socialism in freely held elections? Would it accept such an outcome peacefully? Indeed, if an elected government insisted on carrying out its mandate—which included economic liberalization measures—would the military actually overthrow that government? And what of democracy?

This politico-military situation at the start of the constitutional regime was clearly troubling. If the new democratic regime stood any chance to become consolidated, the elected government needed to send the self-appointed Council of the Revolution back to the barracks. As Larry Graham has astutely observed, "a consolidated democratic regime cannot be achieved without commitment from the military that it will not intervene in politics regardless of electoral outcomes and that it will ignore civilian appeals to the military for assistance on their behalf."[41]

CONCLUSION

In sum, the regime's political challenge involved the need for governmental stability and organizational reach in civil society. The economic challenge demanded that the regime balance the implementation of harsh austerity measures and the promotion of social justice. The military challenge required that the civilian officials assert the supremacy of electoral legitimacy and send the MFA back to the barracks. The study now turns to an analysis of how the new regime confronted its challenges, avoided breakdown and consolidated democracy.

NOTES

1. *Expresso*, 25 July 1976.

2. Further, and for the purposes of conceptual clarity, this book employs a minimalist conception of democracy. Borrowing from Diamond, Linz and Lipset, democracy is defined as a political regime that meets at least three fundamental conditions: (1) the regime has to allow for extensive and realistic competition among either individuals or organized political groups for all positions of power in the government; (2) the regime cannot exclude any major adult group; and (3) civil and political liberties, including all freedoms to compete for political office, such as freedom of assembly, of speech and of movement in society, must be guaranteed. Although other conditions could be added, these three conditions represent the minimal necessary and sufficient conditions for a regime to be considered democratic. See Larry Diamond, Juan J. Linz and Seymour Martin Lipset, eds., *Democracy in Developing Countries: Latin America* (Boulder: Lynne Rienner, 1989), vol. 1, viii–xviii. Also see Joseph A. Schumpeter, *Capitalism, Socialism and Democracy* (New York: Harper Torchbooks, 1962).

3. J. Samuel Valenzuela, "Democratic Consolidation in Post-Transitional Settings: Notion, Process, and Facilitating Conditions," in Scott Mainwaring, Guillermo O'Donnell and J. Samuel Valenzuela, eds., *Issues in Democratic Consolidation: The New South American Democracies in Comparative Perspective* (Notre Dame, IN: University of Notre Dame Press, 1992), 73–94.

4. Samuel P. Huntington, "Will More Countries Become Democratic?" in Samuel P. Huntington and Joseph S. Nye, eds., *Global Dilemmas* (Cambridge, MA: Harvard University Press, 1985), 254–279.

5. See Enrique A. Baloyra, ed., *Comparing New Democracies: Transition and Consolidation in Mediterranean Europe and in the Southern Cone* (Boulder, CO: Westview Press, 1987); Nancy Bermeo, ed., *Liberalization and Democratization: Change in the Soviet Union and Eastern Europe* (Baltimore: Johns Hopkins University Press, 1992); Larry Diamond, "Crisis, Choice and Structure: Reconciling Alternative Models for Explaining Democratic Success and Failure in the Third World." Paper delivered at the 1989 Annual Meeting of the American Political Science Association, Atlanta, 31 August-3 September 1989; Diamond, Linz and Lipset; Samuel P. Huntington, *The Third Wave: Democratization in the Late Twentieth Century* (Norman: University of Oklahoma Press, 1991); Juan Linz and Alfred Stepan, eds. *The Breakdown of Democratic Regimes*, 4 vols. (Baltimore: Johns Hopkins University Press, 1978); Juan Linz and Alfred Stepan, "Political Crafting of Democratic Consolidation or Destruction: European and South American Comparisons," in Robert Pastor, ed., *Democracy in the Americas: Stopping the Pendulum* (New York: Holmes and Meier, 1989); Arturo Valenzuela, *Chile: The Breakdown of Democratic Regimes* (Baltimore: Johns Hopkins University Press, 1978); and idem, "Chile: Origins, Consolidation and Breakdown of a Democratic Regime," in Diamond, Linz and Lipset, *Democracy in Developing Countries,* 157–207.

6. Terry Lynn Karl and Philippe C. Schmitter, "The Conceptual Travels of Transitologists and Consolidologists: How Far to the East Should They Attempt to Go?" *Slavic Review* 53 (Spring 1994): 174–176. See also Nancy Bermeo, "Democracy in Europe," *Daedalus* 123 (Spring 1994): 159–178; Valerie Bunce, "Should Transitologists Be Grounded?" *Slavic Review* 54 (Spring 1995): 111–127.

7. Dankwart Rustow, "Transitions to Democracy: Toward a Dynamic Model," *Comparative Politics* 2 (April 1970): 337–363.

8. Ibid., 358.

9. Ibid.

10. See the discussion by Geoffrey Pridham, "Southern European Democracies on the Road to Consolidation: A Comparative Assessment of the Role of Parties," in Geoffrey Pridham, ed., *Securing Democracy: Political Parties and Democratic Consolidation in Southern Europe* (London: Routledge, 1990), 1–42.

11. Karl and Schmitter, 175.

12. See J. Samuel Valenzuela, 73–94.

13. Among the transitions scholarship on Portugal, see Joaquim Aguiar, "Paradigmas de Decisão Política: Um Modelo de Simulação para Portugal," *Revista de Ciência Política* 3 (Spring 1986): 23–29, and "The Transition to Democracy in Portugal: The New Political Paradigm and the Role of the Communist Party." Paper delivered at the Friedrich Newmann Foundation, Santiago, Chile, December 1988; Nancy Bermeo, *The Revolution Within the Revolution: Workers Control in Rural Portugal* (Princeton: Princeton University Press, 1986); Thomas C. Bruneau, *Politics and Nationhood: Post-Revolutionary Portugal* (New York: Praeger, 1984), and "Discovering Democracy," *The Wilson Quarterly* 9, no. 1 (1985): 67–81; Manuel Braga da Cruz and Miguel Lobo Antunes, "Revolutionary Transition and the Problems of Parliamentary Institutionalization: The Case of the Portuguese National Assembly," in Ulrike Liebert and Maurizio Cotta, eds., *Parliament and Democratic Consolidation in Southern Europe* (London: Pinter, 1990), 154–184; Juan J. Linz, "Spain and Portugal: Critical Choices," in David S. Lander, ed., *Western Europe: The Trials of Partnership* (Lexington, MA: Lexington Books, 1977), 270–285; Paul Manuel, *Uncertain Outcome: The Politics of the Portuguese Transition to Democracy* (Lanham, MD: University Press of America, 1995); Kenneth Maxwell, "Regime Overthrow and the Prospects for Democratic Transition in Portugal," in Guillermo O'Donnell, Philippe C. Schmitter and Lawrence Whitehead, eds., *Transitions from Authoritarian Rule: Southern Europe* (Baltimore: Johns Hopkins University Press, 1986), 109–137; Walter C. Opello, "Portugal's Parliament: An Organizational Analysis of Legislative Performance." *Legislative Studies Quarterly* 11 (August 1986): 291–319.

14. Pridham, 16.

15. Governmental stability was an important issue in the Portuguese consolidation because the country's first experiment with democracy had been a disaster. From 1910 to 1926, parliamentarians had played ministerial musical chairs, eventually resulting in the regime's 1926 breakdown and the imposition of forty-eight years of authoritarianism. The new regime wanted to avoid that fate. See Douglas Wheeler, *Republican Portugal: A Political History, 1910–1926* (Madison: University of Wisconsin Press, 1978), 121–138; A. H. de Oliveira Marques, *A History of Portugal* (New York: Columbia University Press, 1976); Jacques Marcadé, *Le Portugal au XX Siècle, 1910–1985* (Paris: Presses Universitaires de France, 1988).

16. Thomas C. Bruneau, "Political Parties and Democratic Consolidation in Portugal." Paper delivered at the 1990 Annual Meeting of the American Political Science Association, San Francisco, 30 August-2 September 1990, 8–10.

17. See *Constituição da República Portuguesa: As Três Versões Após 25 de Abril 1989/1982/1976* (Lisbon: Porto Editora, 1990), 228–231; David

Corkill, "The Political System and the Consolidation of Democracy in Portugal," *Parliamentary Affairs* (October 1993): 517–532.

18. Due to a legal technicality, the parliament elected in 1976 was comprised of 262 members. See Manuel Cruz and Miguel Lobo Antunes, 180.

19. Thomas C. Bruneau, "Portugal's Unexpected Transition," in Kenneth Maxwell and Michael Haltzel, eds., *Portugal: Ancient Country, Young Democracy* (Washington, D.C.: Woodrow Wilson Center Press, 1990), 9–23; Walter C. Opello, "Portugal," in Vincent C. McHale, ed., *Political Parties of Europe* (Westport, CT: Greenwood Press, 1981), 768–769.

20. Political parties present lists of candidates for office; their preparation is frequently a contentious affair within the parties. Candidates from the Lisbon region often top the list, and the rest of the list typically reflects geographical diversity and party compromises. Often, regions fight to secure their locale a higher position on the list. Parties also seek to list technically competent members high on their lists, so that if they are elected to the National Assembly, these people can help them formulate effective policies. Cruz and Lobo Antunes, 161.

21. These powers are spelled out in articles 150–173. See the *Constituição da República Portuguesa*, 232–235.

22. Opello, "Portugal," 768–769.

23. Ibid., 764–765.

24. See Carlos Gaspar, "Portuguese Communism Since 1976: Limited Decline," *Problems of Communism* 39 (January-February 1990): 45–63.

25. Opello, "Portugal," 756.

26. Daniel H. Levine, "Paradigm Lost: Dependence to Democracy," *World Politics* 2 (April 1988): 377–394.

27. See Gianfranco Pasquino, "Party Elites and Democratic Consolidation: Cross-National Comparisons of Southern European Experiences," in Geoffrey Pridham, ed., *Securing Democracy: Political Parties and Democratic Consolidation in Southern Europe* (New York: Routledge, 1990), 42–62.

28. Adam Przeworski has suggested that a successful consolidation be conceptualized as a situation in which the elite players of the transition agree to the democratic rules of the game and accept the uncertain outcome of the democratic process. Adam Przeworski, "The Games of Transition," in Mainwaring, O'Donnell and Valenzuela, eds., *Issues in Democratic Consolidation: The New South American Democracies in Comparative Perspective* (Notre Dame, IN: University of Notre Dame Press, 1992), 105.

29. Pridham, 10.

30. Levine, 390; Diamond, Linz and Lipset, 35–36; Alfred Stepan, *Rethinking Military Politics* (Princeton: Princeton University Press, 1988), 1–10.

31. Pridham, 26–27.

32. Stuart Holland, "Dependent Development: Portugal as a Periphery," in Dudley Seers, Bernard Schaffer and Marja Liisa Kiljunen, eds., *Underdeveloped Europe: Studies in Core-Periphery Relations* (London: Harvester Press, 1979), 158.

33. See Lawrence S. Graham, "The Military in Politics," in Lawrence S. Graham and Harry M. Makler, eds., *Contemporary Portugal: The Revolution and Its Antecedents* (Austin: University of Texas Press, 1979), 224; Douglas L. Wheeler, "The Honor of the Army," in Graham and Makler, 191–220, and *Republican Portugal.* For theoretical insight into the relationship between the military and politics, see Alfred Stepan, *The Military in Politics* (Princeton: Princeton University Press, 1971).

34. See Marques, 177–224. See also Graham, "The Military in Politics," 224–229. Graham examines the military bureaucracy shaped under Salazar.

35. See Juan Linz, "Totalitarian and Authoritarian Systems," in Fred Greenstein and Nelson Polsby, eds., *Handbook of Social Science*, vol. 3 (Reading, MA: Addison Wesley, 1975), 289.

36. See Manuel.

37. Thomas C. Bruneau, "The Portuguese Coup: Causes and Probable Consequences," *The World Today* (July 1974): 277–288.

38. Pasquino, 212.

39. See *Constituição da República Portuguesa*, 223.

40. Article 143 specifies that the Council of the Revolution is to comprise the President, the Prime Minister (only when a military officer serves as Prime Minister), the heads of the Army, Navy and Air Force, and fourteen lower-ranking officers. Among the Council's leading members were Vítor Alves, Vítor Crespo, Pezerrat Correira and Vasco Lourenço. In his capacity as President, Ramalho Eanes chaired the Council. The lower ranking officers are distributed thus: eight from the Army, three from the Air Force and three from the Navy. See *Constituição da República Portuguesa*, 231.

41. Lawrence Graham, *The Portuguese Military and the State* (Boulder, CO: Westview Press, 1993), 3.

2

The Consolidation's First Period: Political and Economic Instability, 1976–1979

Finally awakening from two years of dizzying political turmoil, the Portuguese body politic began the sober and difficult process of consolidating its new democratic regime in July 1976. The democratic transition had been ideologically polarizing and economically disastrous for Portugal, which contributed to a growing national feeling of discontent during the first few years of the new democratic regime.[1] This chapter conceptualizes the first period of the consolidation process to be when governmental chaos and economic crisis weakened the National Assembly and threatened the young regime's stability, from 1976–1979.

ECONOMIC IMBROGLIO

In an insightful op-ed piece in *Expresso*, Luis Penha Costa declared that economic issues would preoccupy and dominate the agenda of the new constitutional regime. He sarcastically suggested that the revolutionary lyrics in José Alfonso's protest song "Grândola, Vila Morena" ("it is the *people* who give the orders")—which epitomized the hopes of the 25 April 1974 revolution—now be modified to "it is the *economy* that gives the orders."[2]

The economic situation was indeed dire. The costly withdrawal from the former colonies in Africa combined with decreases in remittances from Portuguese emigrants and in tourism income significantly reduced governmental revenues. A 1978 Organization for Economic Cooperation and Development (ODEC) economic survey on Portugal revealed the depth of the economic challenge:

The Portuguese economy has undergone major changes during the last few years. A part of industry and services has been nationalized, a land reform has been introduced, labor relations have been radically altered and a redistribution of income in favor of the lowest wage groups has taken place. In addition, decolonization has brought about a large increase in the population and a loss of traditional markets for Portuguese industries. Besides these specific factors, there have been the effects of the world recession and the relatively slow recovery that followed. The Portuguese economy has therefore been affected by major imbalances with respect to employment, inflation, and the balance of payments.[3]

From 1974 to 1976, per capita income had dropped, capital investment was down and the inflation and unemployment rates had increased. Further, Portugal left the transition period with an overvalued escudo, negative interest rates, and large budget deficits.[4] By 1976, the country had exhausted all of its $2 billion in foreign reserves, and the only significant remaining economic asset was $4 billion in gold reserves that had been stockpiled by the Salazar regime.[5]

THE GOVERNMENTS OF SOCIALIST MINORITY RULE

The First Constitutional Government

On 15 July 1976 President Ramalho Eanes called upon the victor in the April legislative elections, Socialist leader Mário Soares, to form the first constitutional government. Since no single political party had become clearly dominant, the business of governing the new regime was quite complex. Indeed, in spite of his legislative victory, the elections of 25 April 1976 were a disappointment to Mário Soares. In comments he made as a Chubb Fellow at Yale University in January 1976, Soares clearly had anticipated a large Socialist victory, hoping for at least 40 percent of the vote.[6] In addition, during the legislative election campaign, he promised that he would not form a government with any other party. Failing an outright majority, Soares hoped at the very least to lead a strong minority government. The results of the 25 April 1976 legislative voting, however, did not meet his minimum expectations.

As shown in Table 2.1, the Socialist Party lost ground from its 1975 performance in the Constituent Assembly elections, winning nine fewer seats. Its chief opposition, Francisco Sá Carneiro's PSD, also lost some ground, receiving 24.38 percent the vote and seventy-three seats. The two parties at the ideological margins, the PCP and the CDS made significant gains over the results of the 1975 elections. The Social Democratic Center Party (CDS) received 16.0 percent of the vote and forty-two seats. The Communist Party (PC) came in fourth, receiving 14.35 percent of the vote and forty seats. The one remaining seat went to a far-left organization, the Popular Democratic Union (UDP), with 1.69 percent of the vote.[7] A disquieting result for the Socialist Party was that the combined totals for the centrist PPD and the conservative CDS equaled close to 40 percent of the vote, placing Soares and the PS in a generally weak position. Given these electoral results, Soares faced four distinct options regarding the formation of a government.

Soares' first and most logical option was to invite the centrist PSD into a governing coalition. Their combined totals amounted to a strong 55 percent of the vote, and their political programs were only slightly different. In addition, a PS-PSD alliance could provide the regime much-needed stability. However, a governing coalition with the PSD carried a major danger for Soares. The PSD membership drew heavily from center-right *ala liberal* (liberal wing) loyal opposition to the Caetano regime, and in spite of the PS-PSD tactical anti-communist alliance during the transition, many members of the Socialist Party considered the PSD to be too conservative. The danger that a PS-PSD governing alliance could alienate a number of PS deputies—perhaps even lead to a fissure in the party—outweighed the benefits of an alliance with the PSD, so Soares rejected this option.

Table 2.1 Results of the National Assembly Elections of 1975 and 1976

Party	PCP	PS	PPD	CDS
% of Vote in 1975	12.5	37.87	26.4	7.4
Seats Won in 1975	35	116	81	16
% of Vote in 1976	14.35	34.87	24.38	16.00
Seats Won in 1976	40	107	73	42

Note: The PPD later changed its name to PSD. The UDP won a single seat in both elections as well.
Source: Atlas Eleitoral, 1975–1980 (Lisbon: Editorial Progresso Social e Democracia, 1981), 49.

Another option involved an governing alliance with the Communist Party. Álvaro Cunhal, head of the Communist Party, very much wanted to form a leftist government with the Socialists. In Cunhal's view, the PS and PCP combined totals, which represented just under 50 percent of the total vote, could be parlayed into a strong left-wing program. Cunhal and Soares, however, had become bitter rivals during the transition, and did not trust one another. In addition, their legislative goals were quite different. Soares wanted to restore political normalcy, improve the climate for economic growth, and correct the excesses of the revolution. Cunhal called for greater confrontation with the capitalist class. Therefore, Soares refused to form a government with the Communists.

A third option for Soares was to form a government with the Social Democratic Center Party (CDS). Combined, the PS and the CDS represented over 50 percent of the electorate. Led by Diogo Freitas do Amaral, and in spite of its centrist-sounding name, the CDS was a very conservative party, representing many supporters of the Salazar/Caetano regime. The CDS proposed a conservative legislative agenda that included the return of all nationalized properties to their previous owners and the end of socialism. Given their very different legislative agendas, Soares had no interest in forming a government with the CDS.

His fourth and only viable choice was to form a minority Socialist government. After considering his options, and consulting with the President, Soares decided that all of the possible governing coalitions were simply too risky, and formed a Socialist minority government. President Eanes accepted Soares' decision, and has since stated that he was personally convinced in 1976 that the Socialist Party was the only viable political option.[8] The Communists were furious with Soares, but lacked sufficient votes in the National Assembly to stop the formation of a Socialist-led minority government. The CDS and the PSD could have caused the PS some problems, but decided to approve the government. With PS, PSD and CDS support, the National Assembly approved Soares' government on 29 July 1976.[9] Table 2.2 lists the members of this government.

Soares' Legislative Agenda

Upon taking office, the new Prime Minister committed his government to the consolidation of the democratic regime and the construction of socialism. Mário Soares had become Prime Minister in a weakened position, and needed to seek compromises with his conservative opposition. He understood that the key to achieving his twin goals of democratic consolidation and socialism was the restoration of state power and political stability. His legislative package, approved by the National Assembly on 11 August 1976, sought to create a stable climate for economic expansion. Specifically, Soares' plan involved decreasing public expenditures and wages, denationalizing smaller enterprises and increasing some taxes. He identified certain areas of the economy that would remain under the state's control, including banking, insurance, transport and public utilities.

Soares was not giving up on socialism; rather, he was trying to make these state enterprises more efficient and profitable.[10]

Table 2.2 Composition of the First Constitutional Government

Prime Minister	Mário Soares
Minister of State	Henrique de Barros
Minister Without Portfolio	Jorge Campinos
Minister of Foreign Affairs	Medeiros Ferreira
Minister of Defense	Firminio Miguel
Minister of Justice	Almeida Santos
Minister of Internal Affairs	Costa Brás
Minister Economic Cooperation	Sousa Gomes
Minister of Finance	Medina Carreira
Minister of Agriculture and Fisheries	Lopes Cardoso
Minister of Industry and Technology	Walter Rosa
Minister of Business and Tourism	António Barreto
Minister of Urban Housing and Construction	Eduardo Pereira
Minister of Labor	Marcelo Curto
Minister of Social Affairs	Armando Bacelar
Minister of Education and Scientific Investigations	Sottomayor Cardia

Source: História Contemporânea de Portugal (Lisbon: Amigos do Livro, 1985).

Interestingly, during the early days of this government an operational PS-PSD majority emerged. Soares' legislative program, rejected by the PC and the CDS, passed thanks to the support of the PS and PSD deputies. On the left, the Communist Party condemned this legislative program as a step toward the recovery by the capitalist classes of their former position in Portuguese society; on the right, the CDS viewed this program as tilting the country in the direction of socialism.[11] The PS and PSD found common ground, which provided some governmental stability.

Soares also wanted to restore law and order in the Alentejo and Ribatejo regions. Considered by many as the penultimate example of excess during the revolutionary period, landless farm workers had appropriated over 2 million acres of land from plantation owners between 11 March and 25 November 1975. These landless peasants, often led by PCP or far-leftist operatives, converted the land into collective farms. By and large these collectives were unprofitable, and the former owners were not compensated for their losses.[12]

The Socialist Minister of Agriculture, António Lopes Cardoso, ordered the eviction of these illegal occupants of plantations. As the police moved in, peasants resisted, and there were numerous clashes between them. Lopes Cardoso, who identified himself with the PS's radical left, resigned in protest over Soares' policies. This prompted a political crisis for Soares, who replaced Lopes Cardoso with António Barreto. The new Agricultural Minister pledged to maintain the government's land reform program, albeit with some revisions.[13]

The Socialist government also wanted to break Communist domination of the trade union movement. It rescinded the *unicidade* law, passed in 1975, which had permitted only Communist organization of the workforce, and encouraged Socialist workers to engage in a letter-writing campaign known as the open letter *(carta aberta)* program, aimed at dislodging Communists from leadership positions. However, the Communists had already established a tight, disciplined labor organization, the National Confederation of Portuguese Workers-National Intersyndical (CGTP-Inter), which had contained over 1 million workers and represented 149 of the 293 unions in Portugal. For three years Socialists tried in vain to oust the Communist leadership. Exasperated, they gave up their *carta aberta* strategy in 1979 and formed a rival organization, known as the General Union of Workers or UGT (União Geral dos Trabalhadores). This Socialist-dominated union had contained some 500,000 members in forty unions.[14]

Resistance from the Far Left. Predictably, Soares encountered a great amount of resistance from the far left. They were upset not only by his legislative agenda but also by his lenient treatment of former regime supporters. For instance, when the exiled rightist General António de Spínola returned to Portugal from Brazil on 10 August 1976, and was jailed, government officials released him the next day.[15] Officials also reduced the prison terms of many officers of the former state police, PIDE/DGS. In 1978, President Eanes allowed the former President, eighty-three-year-old General Américo Tómas, to return to Portugal from exile. These decisions infuriated the far left, who felt that no sympathy should be given to these hated members of the former regime.

Perhaps no decision perturbed Soares' opposition more than when, in January 1977, the administration stated that it wanted to rebuild the former monopoly group, *Companhia União Fabril* (CUF). Before the 25 April 1974 revolution the CUF, which consisted of Portugal's seven largest financial institutions (Espírito Santo, Banco Português do Atlântico, Champlamaud, Fonsecas and Burnay, Nacional Ultramarino and Borges and Irmão), had controlled close to three-fourths of the gross national product. Nationalizations of their properties in March 1975 by the MFA government was considered to be a great revolutionary advance.[16] The Socialist government argued that a reconstituted CUF would help Portugal become more competitive with the world's leading capitalist nations. Soares traveled to Brazil in 1976 to ask some 30,000 self-exiled Portuguese businessmen to return home.[17]

Outraged, Álvaro Cunhal lambasted Soares at the November 1976 Party Congress, accusing him of turning the country back to the reactionaries. Subsequently, the General Confederation of Portuguese Workers (Confederação Geral dos Trabalhadores Portugueses-CGTP) organized massive anti-Soares demonstrations all over the country, leading to an increase in social tension and a general feeling of uncertainty.[18] In addition, the return of over 600,000 Portuguese citizens from Portugal's former colonies—known as the *retornados*—placed great stress on governmental services. Many of these people were forced to leave Africa hastily, so they arrived penniless and homeless. The government set up large tent cities in the suburban areas around Lisbon, and asked family members to take in their relatives. These living conditions led to an increase in crime in the urban areas outside of Lisbon.[19]

The discontent of the far left also manifested itself in a number of bombings throughout the period. For instance, in Lisbon, there were bomb blasts outside the Sheraton and Ritz hotels, symbols of American luxury and capitalism.[20] Other bombings occurred at a bank, a movie theater, a subway station and government land-reform centers in the Alentejo;[21] one attack disrupted the Lisbon water supply.[22] Fortunately, there were no injuries in any of these cases, but the government was unable to stop the activity.

Many of Soares' leftist opponents felt that he was a pawn of the United States, arguing that during the transition CIA operatives, aided by Soares and others, penetrated and destroyed the revolutionary process in progress (known as the PREC).[23] These groups tried to discredit Soares again when, during a October 1976 Presidential debate in the United States on foreign policy, President Gerald Ford stated to Jimmy Carter that the defeat of Communists and other leftists in Portugal was a foreign policy success for his administration. Soares' opponents heralded Ford's comments as a confession that the United States had illegally intervened in the transition, and hoped to use this to delegitimize the new constitutional regime. Not everyone in Portugal agreed with Ford, however. Whereas the Communist media, led by *O Diário* called this revelation shocking, the more conservative press dismissed Ford's comments.[24] *O Dia*, for instance, argued that Portuguese democracy was the result of the firm determination of the Portuguese people, not of American foreign policy. Ford's comments angered Communists and other leftists, but did not significantly undermine the legitimacy of the new constitutional regime.[25]

Soares encountered some left-wing opposition within his own party as well. At the Socialist Party meeting on 1 November 1976, Aires Rodriques and Carmalinda Perreira—two Socialist deputies who had voted against Soares' legislative program—argued that Soares had adopted a much too conservative path. After Soares defended his policies as the only realistic path available, the membership reelected him leader of the Socialist Party with 75 percent of the votes, and expelled Rodriques and Perreira from the party. The two of them stayed in the National Assembly under the banner of their newly formed party, the Unified Socialist Working Party. A few days later the former Minister of Agriculture, António Lopes Cardoso, announced that he too was leaving the Socialist Party, retaining his National Assembly seat, and forming a party called the Union of the Left.[26]

Given the general political and economic turmoil, the scheduled 12 December 1976 municipal elections assumed great importance. Even though the Socialist government did not need to win these elections to remain in power, Mário Soares stated that he would respect the outcome, and frame his political agenda accordingly. Soares' wager paid off. As shown in Table 2.3, the Socialists won 33.22 percent of the vote, and demonstrated that their support had not significantly eroded during the five months of their rule. Further, the party demonstrated nationwide strength, winning the Lisbon, Faro, Oporto and Coimbra city halls. The PSD remained the second strongest party, polling best in the islands. The PCP maintained a strong position in the Alentejo, and the CDS scored some victories in the North.

Table 2.3 Results of the Municipal Elections of 12 December 1976

Party	PCP	PS	PPD	CDS
% of Vote	17.69	33.22	24.28	16.61
City Halls Won	37	115	115	36
City Councils Won	38	111	118	36
Local Councils Won	195	1,113	1,262	533

Note: The PPD later changed its name to PSD.
Source: Atlas Eleitoral, 1975–1980 (Lisbon: Editorial Progresso Social e Democracia, 1981).

Although the elections helped stabilize Socialist leadership, the economy showed few signs of improvement. Rather than impose even more austere measures on the people, Soares tried to alleviate the economic situation by borrowing money from other countries and from the International Monetary Fund (IMF). In December 1976 the United States loaned Portugal $300 million, followed by a June 1977 loan of $750 million from a group of fourteen countries, organized by President Carter. These loans were, in part, secured by a percentage of Portugal's gold reserves, and conditional upon the implementation of an austerity program.[27] They stabilized the immediate economic situation but did not lead to any real improvements in the economy. For long-term economic help, Portugal formally applied to join the European Economic Community (EEC) in 1977.

The President and the Prime Minister

The dual executive arrangement embodied in the new constitutional regime obliged the Prime Minister to function under the general auspices of the President. Elected by over 60 percent of the vote in the June presidential election, President Ramalho Eanes represented a stabilizing political force for the young regime. In his inaugural address, Eanes had committed himself to overseeing the peaceful consolidation of democracy in Portugal, and promised that his administration would oppose any and all groups that attempted to overthrow the rule of law.[28]

President Eanes accepted Soares' decisions to obtain the loans, but was very concerned that in the long run this use of the gold reserves would compromise national independence. As such, President Eanes insisted that the government should adopt harsh austerity measures in order to pay off the loans as soon as feasible. Following Eanes' directives, Soares announced on 25 February 1977 a series of austerity measures. Among other steps, these measures provided for a 15 percent devaluation of the escudo, an increase in import surcharges, and new incentives for emigrant workers to send money home.[29] In addition, Eanes pressed Soares to make some cabinet changes. On 26 March 1977, Soares accepted the President's demands, and appointed two technocrats to his administration: Alfredo Nobre da Costa as the Minister of Industry, and Carlos Mota Pinto as Minister of Tourism. These decisions were warmly greeted by the PSD and the CDS.[30]

An unforeseen institutional problem for Soares in his decision to govern from a minority position was that each time his government stalemated with the National Assembly, power and authority shifted to the President. Whenever his government faced a crisis, the President stepped in and restored order. After two years of Socialist minority rule and general governmental instability, President Eanes became widely perceived as the savior of the democratic system from the political parties. Mário Soares has remarked that, in retrospect, his decision to form a minority government may have been the greatest political mistake of his career. If he had formed a center-left governing coalition with the PSD in 1976, his government not only could have avoided some of the periods of instability in 1977 and 1978, but also could have kept the President from intervening in the National Assembly.[31]

The Collapse of the First Constitutional Government

By June 1977 it had become evident that Soares' polices were failing: the key economic indicators of inflation, unemployment and the balance of payment had not improved.[32] Given this developing crisis of authority, President Eanes stated that he would not stand by and let the political and economic situation crumble, declaring in a speech commemorating the 25 April 1974 Revolution: "My mandate from the Portuguese people obliges me to ensure national recovery, national identity and relief of the country's anguish about the present and future. I shall not hesitate to take necessary, correct steps, within a democratic framework, to ensure the viability of this nation as a society worth living in."[33]

Desperate to stabilize the economy, Prime Minister Soares turned to the International Monetary Fund (IMF). After several months of tedious negotiations, the IMF granted Portugal a $7.5 million loan, conditional upon a number of harsh austerity measures. Finalized in October 1977, the IMF deal was poorly received in Portugal. Critics claimed that Soares had humiliated the nation by accepting the IMF conditions, and demanded his ouster. In response, Soares called for a vote of no confidence, which he lost by a 159–100 margin in December 1977.[34]

At that point President Eanes faced three options. He could dissolve the National Assembly and call for new elections, he could appoint a new Prime Minister, or he could ask Soares to form a new government. He chose the third option, and suggested that Soares form a government with Franciso Sá Carneiro. In his view, a PS-PSD governing alliance would provide a majoritarian government and the stability needed for democratic consolidation and economic recovery. In retrospect, Eanes was absolutely correct that the most logical governing coalition was between the PS and the PSD, but an increasingly bad personal relationship between Soares and Sá Carneiro precluded that possibility.[35] Soares wanted to return to power, but since a PS-PSD government was not a viable option at that time, he had to consider an alliance with the PCP or the CDS.

There was an ideological rationale for a PS-PCP governing alliance in that the Socialists and the Communists agreed in a very broad way on the need for socialism. However, Soares rejected that option based on his personal rivalry with Álvaro Cunhal and on his view that the PCP was a dangerous, anti-democratic party.

The only remaining alternative was to form an alliance with the conservative CDS party. On the face of it, a PS-CDS government made absolutely no sense, since these two parties disagreed in almost every area of policy and ideology. As such, the country was stunned when Soares announced on 27 January 1978 that he and CDS head Diogo Freitas do Amaral had agreed to terms on the formation of a PS-CDS government.[36]

The Second Constitutional Government

This arrangement clearly was politically motivated, reminiscent of the old adage that politics makes strange bedfellows. Soares wanted to remain in power, and Freitas do Amaral sought to elevate his party to greater credibility. Their joint legislative program sought to implement the IMF austerity program. In return for its support, the CDS received the ministries of Foreign Affairs, International Trade and Administrative Reform.[37] After they presented the terms of their agreement to President Eanes—who accepted this government—the National Assembly approved the second constitutional government with the support of the PS and CDS deputies. The second constitutional government is listed in Table 2.4.

Table 2.4 Composition of the Second Constitutional Government

Prime Minister	Mário Soares
Adjunct Prime Minister	Almeida Santos
Minister of Foreign Affairs	Sá Machado
Minister of Defense	Firmínio Miguel
Minister of Justice	Santos Pais
Minister of Administrative Reform	Rui Pena
Minister of Finance and Planning	Vitor Constâncio
Minister of Agriculture and Fisheries	Luis Saias
Minister of Industry and Technology	Carlos Melancia
Minister of Business and Tourism	Basílio Horta
Minister of Urban Habitation and Construction	Sousa Gomes
Minister of Transportation and Communications	Ferreira Lima
Minister of Labor	Maldnado Gonelha
Minister of Social Affairs	António Arnault
Minister of Education and Scientific Investigations	Sottomayor Cardia

Source: História Contemporânea de Portugal (Lisbon: Amigos do Livro, 1985).

The PS-CDS government sent shock waves through the PSD membership, who felt that Sá Carneiro's confrontational approach to the PS had cost them a chance to govern. At the February PSD party conference in Oporto, tensions escalated, and Sá Carneiro resigned his post as party leader. The issue of whether to work with the Socialists or confront them had badly divided the PSD. Sá Carneiro returned to his leadership post later in the year, but the PSD remained divided.[38]

The PS-CDS government did not work very well.[39] In a 1980 interview with the *Diário de Noticias*, Freitas do Amaral observed that the only point of agreement between the PS and CDS was the initial accord to implement the IMF austerity program, and to continue negotiations with the EEC regarding Portugal's application for entry. From that point forward, the PS and the CDS could not agree on policy. Amaral described sharing power with the PS as a negative and frustrating experience, asserting that the PS used the CDS to promote a more centrist image while pursuing an extreme leftist policy with the PCP.[40] It is difficult to assess Amaral's statement that a PS-PCP secret accord existed, but it is certainly true that the PS-CDS second constitutional government did not work very well. Economic problems and social agitation continued, and by August right-wing CDS members demanded that the party leave the government. Having realized few fruits from its role in the government, and risking party defections, the CDS pulled out of the alliance in August, forcing the government's collapse.[41]

The End of Socialist Minority Rule

The collapse of the PS-CDS government led to a major battle between Eanes and Soares. Eanes wanted Soares to resign, so that he could help organize a stable, majority government. It appeared that the President wanted to fashion a PS-PSD government, and reappoint Soares as Prime Minister. Soares, however, did not accept Eanes' right to intervene in the process without the National Assembly specifically giving the Prime Minister a vote of no confidence. Since the CDS ministers had resigned, but there had not been a vote of no confidence, Soares felt that he had every right to continue to lead the government. In fact, it seems as if Soares hoped that the National Assembly would again accept Socialists' governing from a minority position.

Given Soares' refusal to cooperate with the President, Eanes was left with few options. Without the Socialists, he could not frame a majority government. Further, since legislative elections were already scheduled for 1980, Eanes did not think that anticipating those elections would contribute to a stable political and economic environment.[42] Having no other viable option, the President named an industrialist with no official party affiliation, Alfredo Nobre da Costa, to be the new Prime Minister. He hoped that Nobre da Costa would remain the Prime Minister until the scheduled legislative elections. This intervention by Eanes into the affairs of the National Assembly greatly angered Soares, and was the beginning of an intense personal rivalry between the two men.

THE GOVERNMENTS OF PRESIDENTIAL MEDIATION

The Third Constitutional Government

Alfredo Nobre da Costa assumed office on 29 August 1978, and faced a very difficult task. As an independent, he had no automatic base of support in the National Assembly, and deputies deeply resented Eanes' imposition of this government. For the sake of governmental stability, the National Assembly approved his technocratic cabinet, but that turned out to be the only positive vote received by this government. Table 2.5 lists the third constitutional government.

Nobre da Costa sought drastic budgetary cuts to quickly implement the terms of the IMF agreement. His economic program—criticized by deputies as extremist—was rejected by the National Assembly just seventeen days into his administration, forcing Nobre da Costa to resign. He agreed to stay on as Prime Minister until a replacement was found.[43]

Table 2.5 Composition of the Third Constitutional Government

Prime Minister	Nobre da Costa
Adjunct Prime Minister	Costa Freitas
Minister of Foreign Affairs	Correira Gago
Minister of Defense	Firminio Miguel
Minister of Justice	Mário Raposo
Minister of Internal Administration	Gonçalves Ribeiro
Minister of Finance and Planning	Silva Lopes
Minister of Agriculture and Fisheries	Vaz Portugal
Minister of Industry and Technology	Santos Martins
Minister of Business and Tourism	Pires de Miranda
Minister of Urban Habitation and Construction	Almeida Pina
Minister of Transportation and Communications	Amílcar Gouveia Marques
Minister of Labor	Costa Leal
Minister of Social Affairs	Acácio Magro
Minister of Education and Culture	Lloyd Braga

Source: História Contemporânea de Portugal (Lisbon: Amigos do Livro, 1985).

With the fall of the third constitutional government, the political situation was again in the hands of President Eanes. He sought a Prime Minister who could hold a government together until the scheduled parliamentary elections in 1980. After almost a month of consultations, Eanes appointed University of Coimbra law professor Alberto Mota Pinto as Premier on 25 October 1978.[44] Mota Pinto was an independent, but unlike Nobre da Costa, he was connected to a political party. In 1975–1976, he had been the PSD floor leader in the Constituent Assembly; he left the party following a personal dispute with Sá Carneiro. The PS and the CDS found Mota Pinto to be an acceptable choice. The PSD had some reservations about the appointment, but withheld judgment until he submitted his political proposals. The PCP considered the choice to be too conservative. With the support of the PS and the CDS, the Mota Pinto government was approved by the National Assembly on 12 December 1978.[45]

The Fourth Constitutional Government

Listed in Table 2.6, Mota Pinto's government was decidedly rightist. His legislative agenda proposed, among other items, to implement the IMF austerity

Table 2.6 Composition of the Fourth Constitutional Government

Prime Minister	Mota Pinto
Deputy Prime Minister and European Integration	Jacinto Nunes
Adjunct Prime Minister	Álvaro Monjardino
Minister of Foreign Affairs	Freitas Cruz
Minister of Defense	Loureiro dos Santos
Minister of Justice	Eduardo Correira
Minister of Internal Administration	Gonçalves Ribeiro
Minister of Finance and Planning	Jacinto Nunes
Minister of Agriculture and Fisheries	Vaz Portugal
Minister of Industry andTechnology	Álvaro Barreto
Minister of Business and Tourism	Repolho Correira
Minister of Housing and Construction	Almeida Pina
Minister of Transportation and Communications	Marques da Costa
Minister of Labor	Eusébio de Carvalho
Minister of Social Affairs	Acácio Magro
Minister of Education and Culture	Valente de Oliveira

Source: História Contemporânea de Portugal (Lisbon: Amigos do Livro, 1985).

measures, redefining the public/private areas of the state, cutting back on nationalized industries and hastening the return of Alentejo lands to their former owners.

Astonished at the conservative tone and direction of this program, Mário Soares called this the most right-wing government since before the 25 April revolution.[46] Agreeing, Communist head Álvaro Cunhal demanded that this legislative agenda be defeated by the parties of the left, and his appeal found resonance among many Socialist deputies. Allied, the PCP and PS had the votes to stop this program. Yet a PS-PCP alliance did not emerge. Arguing that the best way to delegitimize the right was to let their policy proposals fail on their own, Soares ordered the Socialist deputies to abstain on the vote to approve Mota Pinto's legislative package. At the root of this decision was the fact that Soares did not trust Cunhal, and feared that his party might lose its identity if it confronted the CDS-PSD-Eanes alliance with the support of the Communist Party. Soares' decision enabled Mota Pinto's program to pass by a 109–47 margin, with 97 abstentions: the PSD and the CDS voted in favor, the PCP against, and the PS abstained.[47]

Bolstered by the vote, Mota Pinto started to govern. He implemented his program, continued negotiations with the European Community and hastened the return of lands in the Alentejo. He was a competent Prime Minister, and it appeared that he would be able to govern until the 1980 National Assembly elections. Unexpectedly, however, the PSD forced his government's collapse. Francisco Sá Carneiro ordered the PSD to abstain on the April vote on Mota Pinto's budget. Without PSD support, it was rejected by the National Assembly, obliging him to resign.[48]

On the face of it, Sá Carnerio's decision made no sense. Mota Pinto had proposed a conservative budget and sought to implement much of what the PSD itself had proposed. However, Sá Carneiro was not driven by policy in this case, but by his own political ambition. If the government's conservative budget had been successful, Mota Pinto would have received the credit, and have been well positioned for the 1980 legislative elections. Sensing the rightward trend of the country, Sá Carneiro wanted to force a governmental crisis so that Eanes would call for new legislative elections. He anticipated that the PSD could win those elections, and that he would become the conservative Prime Minister.

This strategy, however, was not without its costs. Sá Carneiro's decision to bring about the collapse of the Mota Pinto government led to a mutiny within the PSD ranks. Many members felt that Sá Carneiro had no right to abstain on a budget consistent with PSD policy. Claiming that his own ambition—and not the interest of the party—motivated Sá Carneiro, thirty-seven members of the PSD delegation left the party but remained in the National Assembly under a new party banner, called the Independent Social Democratic Assembly.[49] Soares immediately made overtures to these dissident PSD members in an effort to form a new majority government. President Eanes, however, had decided that the only way out of political instability was to hold interim elections, and announced that elections would take place in December.

Divergent Presidential and Parliamentary Conceptions

President Ramalho Eanes' bold but controversial step to call for interim elections, warmly greeted by Sá Carneiro, was yet another source of bad blood between Soares and Eanes. Eanes considered it to be a responsible presidential act, whereas Soares considered this intervention both unnecessary and unwarranted. Carlos Gaspar has perceptively observed that the Eanes-Soares conflict involved "two distinct conceptions of the political system—a parliamentary versus a presidential conception—more than a deliberate clash between conflicting strategies."[50] Indeed, the country's dual executive system was at the center of the struggle between Eanes and Soares.

President Eanes felt that he represented a national constituency, and argued that the President, as stabilizer of the political system, should control major national policy decisions. For Eanes, presidentialism implied the ability for one democratically elected leader to rise above the narrow interests of parties, and seek out technically competent people to address the nation's problems.

Admitting that presidentialism could provide political stability in the short term, Soares became convinced that one of the causes of the persistent governmental instability had become the very interventions of President Eanes in the legislative process. In his view, it was not necessary for a President to step in every time the National Assembly deadlocked: if given a sufficient chance, the government could right itself and provide a stable, democratic political leadership. Soares believed that the National Assembly was the most representative and democratic institutional arrangement possible, and, as the laboratory of Portuguese democracy, should be primary in the democratic system.

Complicating the Eanes-Soares relationship were rumors that the President intended to form his own party to support his presidentialist vision in the National Assembly. In an interview with the *New York Times*, Soares expressed his frustration with the President: "What is grave is that the President neither wants to take the risks of being in a presidential system nor does he allow the parliamentary system to govern. That is the impasse."[51]

CONCLUSION

After three years of weak governments in the National Assembly, the young democracy appeared to be very far from dealing with its political, economic and military challenges. Mário Soares had learned that it is very difficult to govern from a minority position, and the relationship between the two leading politicians of the period, Eanes and Soares, had deteriorated. As Portugal prepared for its 1979 interim parliamentary elections, the uncertain political and economic situations imperiled the consolidation of the new regime.

NOTES

1. Terry Lynn Karl and Philippe Schmitter have observed that the transition's "extensive nationalizations of industry and expropriations of land . . . rendered the subsequent consolidation of democracy . . . difficult." Terry Lynn Karl and Philippe Schmitter, "Modes of Transition in Latin America, Southern and Eastern Europe," *International Social Science Journal* 128 (May 1991): 269–284.

2. *Expresso*, 9 July 1976.

3. *OECD Economic Survey: Portugal* (Washington, D.C.: OECD, 1978), 1.

4. Christine A. Bogdanowicz-Bindert, "Portugal, Turkey and Peru: Three Successful Stabilization Programs Under the Auspices of the IMF," *World Development* 2, no. 1 (1993): 65–70.

5. Ibid. See also Jorge Braga de Macedo and Simon Serfaty, eds. *Portugal Since the Revolution: Economic and Political Perspectives* (Boulder, CO: Westview Press, 1981); Jorge Braga de Macedo, "*A Constituição e a Economia: Como Superar o Bloqueio.*" Paper delivered at the conference "The Constitution and the Consolidation of Democracy in Portugal, 1976–1989", Camões Center, Columbia University, 10 November 1989; Anthony S. Courakis, Fátima Moura-Roque and George Tridimas, "Public Expenditures and Growth in Greece and Portugal: Wagner's Law and Beyond," *Applied Economics* 25 (1993): 125–134.

6. *New York Times*, 23 January 1976.

7. *Atlas Eleitoral 1975–1980* (Lisbon: Editorial Progresso Social e Democracia, 1981), 49.

8. Interview with Ramalho Eanes, *Diário de Notícias*, 24 April 1984.

9. The 23 July 1976 edition of *Expresso* reported that the National Assembly at São Bento took up the issues of its organization and procedural rules. In the first few weeks of its inaugural session, it debated and passed over 170 articles regarding its internal structure, organization and procedures. The Assembly decided to create eleven committees, and set one-fourth of the total members present as the minimum for a quorum. The committees formed were Constitutional Affairs; Civil Liberties and Rights; Labor; Social Security and Health; Education; Science and Culture; Economy, Finances and Planning; Agriculture and Fisheries; National Defense; Foreign Affairs and Emigration; Internal Administration and Local Power. See also Manuel Braga da Cruz and Miguel Lobo Antunes, "Revolutionary Transition and the Problems of Parliamentary Institutionalization," in Ulrike Liebert and Maurizio Cotto, eds.,

Parliament and Democratic Consolidation in Southern Europe (London: Pinter, 1990), 167.

10. All of the Lisbon dailies were full of reports on Soares' legislative program. Among others, see reports of 11–14 August 1976 in *Diário de Notícias*.

11. See the political analysis by Joaquim Aguiar, *A Ilusão do Poder: Análise do Sistema Partidário Português, 1976–1982* (Lisbon: Dom Quixote, 1982).

12. Walter C. Opello, *Portugal: From Monarchy to Pluralist Democracy* (Boulder, CO: Westview Press, 1991), 102–105.

13. This crisis forced Soares to cancel a trip to a Socialist International meeting in the Netherlands, where he would have been heralded as a hero in the international Socialist movement. This was a major story in the Lisbon dailies. See coverage in the first two weeks of November 1976 in *Diário de Notícias, O Dia*, and the 5 November and 12 November 1976 editions of *Expresso*.

14. See discussion by J. Samuel Valenzuela, "Labor Movements in Transitions to Democracy: A Framework for Analysis," *Comparative Politics* 21, no. 4 (July 1989): 445–472; Thomas C. Bruneau and Alex MacCleod, *Politics in Contemporary Portuga*l (Boulder, CO: Lynne Rienner, 1986), 105–106; Martin Kayman, *Revolution and Counterrevolution in Portugal* (London: Merlin Press, 1987), 195.

15. *Expresso*, 12 August 1976.

16. Miguel Rodrigues Pintado and Alvaro Mendonça, *Os Novos Grupos Económicos* (Lisbon: Texto Editora, 1989), 13–31.

17. *Diário de Notícias,* 30 January 1977.

18. Ibid., 15 January 1977.

19. Remarkably, in a few years all of the *retornados* were absorbed into society, typically thanks to family members.

20. *Diário de Notícias*, 15 October 1976.

21. Ibid., 9 September 1976; 16 November 1976.

22. Ibid., 12 October 1976.

23. PREC stands for "Processo Revolucionário em Curso."

24. See *Diário de Notícias and O Diário*, 7–10 November 1976.

25. *Diário de Notícias*, 9 October 1976.

26. Cruz and Antunes, 180.

27. Bogdanowicz-Bindert, 66.

28. See Mário Soares, *Vencer a Crise: Um Ano de Governo Constitucional* (Lisbon: Secretaria de Estado da Comunicação Social, 1977).

29. See useful report in *Facts on File*, 30 April 1977, 330.

30. Nobre da Costa had a background in the development of oil, and Mota Pinto was a professor of commercial law at the University of Coimbra. Mota Pinto replaced Francisco Marcelo Curto, who had angered labor and management by slow responses to requests. These changes are reported in *Facts on File*, 30 April 1977, 330.

31. Bruneau and MacCleod, 65.

32. *Diário de Notícias*, 28 March 1977. Also see 15 May 1977 report in *Facts on File*, 197734.

33. *Facts on File*, 30 April 1977, 330.

34. Carlos Gaspar, "Constitutional Politics and Regime Stability," in Kenneth R. Maxwell and Scott C. Monje, eds., *Portugal: The Constitution and the Consolidation of Democracy, 1976–1989* (New York: Camões Center, Columbia University, 1991), 33.

35. In a 6 January 1979 interview with *Expresso*, "Mário Soares e Eu Somos e Seremos Adversários Políticos," Francisco Sá Carneiro stated that he and Mário Soares were, and would always be, political adversaries.

36. *Diário de Notícias*, 28 January 1978.

37. See the 21 January 1978 political analysis in *Expresso* by Marcelo Rebelo de Sousa, "41 Meses Depois e o CDS é Governo."

38. *Expresso*, 4 February 1978.

39. See *Expresso*, 11 March 1978. In particular, Marcelo Rebelo de Sousa's story on the dilemas of austerity, "Salario ou Emprego: Dilema da Austeridade," is worth reading.

40. Interview with Freitas do Amaral, *Diário de Notícias*, 9 September 1980.

41. *Diário de Notícias*, 25 July 1978.

42. Opello, 106; Gaspar, 34.

43. *Diário de Notícias*, 15 September 1978.

44. Opello, 106; Kayman, 205–206.

45. *Expresso*, 12 December 1978.

46. Kayman, 205.

47. *Expresso*, 12 December 1978.

48. *Diário de Notícias*, 6–7 June 1979.

49. Opello, 107.

50. Gaspar, 33.

51. *New York Times*, 26 July 1979.

3

The Consolidation's Second Period: The National Assembly Resolves the Military Challenge, 1979–1983

The consolidation's second period may be conceptualized as that span of time when the National Assembly effectively asserted its authority over the military challenge. This chapter examines how the emergence of the conservative Democratic Alliance in the 1979 interim elections led to the elimination of the Council of the Revolution in 1982, significantly advancing the regime's prospects for consolidation.

CONFRONTING THE MILITARY CHALLENGE

An institutional legacy of the transitional period, the Council of the Revolution (CR), granted itself complete control over the military and maintained the right to veto any legislation it considered unconstitutional. The only way to eliminate the CR from the political game was to amend the Constitution. However, there were two major problems involved in a constitutional revision. First, the large amount of governmental instability in the regime's first three years of existence made it very difficult for any of the governments to focus on a constitutional revision. Second, and perhaps more important, not all of the elected officials considered it necessary to abolish the CR. President Eanes, a military man, chaired the Council, and did not readily perceive a problem in its cohabitation with the democratic regime. In addition, Mário Soares did not appear to view the Council as inherently antidemocratic. The Communist Party and other far-left parties were among the Council's biggest supporters. In general, the left viewed the CR with sympathy and supported its commitment to the construction of socialism by democratic means.

Not surprisingly, it was the non-Socialist political parties that objected most strenuously to the leftist CR and sought its abolition. The PSD and the CDS argued that the Constitution was inherently undemocratic, in that it both imposed socialism as the telos of the Portuguese state and provided for a military council to ensure that the transition to socialism was successful. CDS head Diogo Freitas do Amaral aptly summed up the problem:

> . . . in the years from 1976 to 1979, the role of the Council of the Revolution was not unanimously perceived by public opinion as negative because the governments issued from elections at that time were mainly governments of the left or center-left. They were, therefore, seen with a certain degree of sympathy by the military left, which formed the majority of the Council of the Revolution, so the Council did not make a lot of trouble for them. But when the so-called Democratic Alliance—a center-right coalition of Social Democrats and Christian Democrats—won the 1979 general elections with an absolute majority and began to try to implement its own program along more conservative lines, the conflict with the Council of the Revolution became apparent to all.[1]

As the 1979 electoral campaign got under way, this military issue became more important. Since, for the most part, the left seemed comfortable with the Council of the Revolution and the wording of the Constitution, it was up to the center and the right-wing parties to force the issue.

A CARETAKER GOVERNMENT

The Fifth Constitutional Government

In the meantime, President Eanes appointed Maria de Loudres Pintasilgo as the new Prime Minister to maintain governmental stability during the electoral campaign. Pintasilgo, a radical Catholic Socialist, had been Portugal's delegate to UNESCO in Paris. This caretaker appointment was widely interpreted as Eanes' gesture to the left, partly in response to vociferous criticisms of his decision to dissolve the Socialist-led National Assembly.

Apparently two members of the Council of the Revolution, Vítor Alves and Melo Antunes, had pushed Eanes to appoint Pintasilgo as part of a larger strategy to attract voters to the left by the novelty of a Catholic, Socialist woman Prime Minister.[2] The right did not support the appointment, but since it was a caretaker government, and they needed to prepare for elections, Pintasilgo's cabinet was quickly approved. Her government is listed in Table 3.1.

Governing under the shadow of the larger national political dynamic, Maria de Lourdes Pintasilgo assumed office with the statement that "it is with hope that I start this 100 day march."[3] As Prime Minister, she stabilized national leadership, continued to abide by the IMF agreements, and provided some relief to working families. There was a moderate increase in the minimum wage, and increases in retirement and unemployment benefits.[4] In a 1980 interview with the *Diário de Notícias*, she stated that the greatest accomplishment of her term of office was "the protection of the poorest members of the society."[5]

Table 3.1 Composition of the Fifth Constitutional Government

Prime Minister	Maria de Lourdes Pintasilgo
Minister of Foreign Affairs	Freitas Cruz
Minister of Defense	Loureiro dos Santos
Minister of Justice	Sousa Macedo
Minister of Internal Administration	Costa Brás
Minister of Economic Planning and Coordination	Correira Gago
Minister of Finance	Sousa Franco
Minister of Agriculture and Fisheries	Joaquim Lourenco
Minister of Industry andTechnology	Fernando Marques Videira
Minister of Business and Tourism	Pereira Magro
Minister of Habitation and Construction	Mario de Azevedo
Minister of Transportation and Communications	Monteiro da Silva
Minister of Labor	Sá Borges
Minister of Social Affairs	Alfredo Bruto da Costa
Minister of Education	Veiga da Cunha
Minister of Culture and Science	Sedas Nunes
Minister of Social Communication	João Figueiredo

Source: História Contemporânea de Portugal (Lisbon, Amigos do Livro, 1985).

THE ELECTORAL CYCLE OF 1979–1980

The decision by President Eanes to have interim legislative elections in 1979 initiated an electoral cycle: municipal elections also were scheduled for 1979, followed by the regularly scheduled 1980 legislative elections and the Presidential election. The hope was that by the end of 1980, all of these elections would have clarified the political situation.[6]

The 1979 Legislative Campaign

Francisco Sá Carneiro sensed that these interim elections were his chance to take advantage of the frustration people were feeling after three years of governmental and economic instability. In particular, many moderate supporters of Mário Soares and the PS were disappointed with their two years of rule, and appeared to be looking for new answers. Sá Carneiro's close associate, Francisco

Pinto Balsemão, astutely described this generalized feeling of frustration in an interview with the *New York Times*, noting that "[in Portugal] . . . we have been living in a society which has one foot in a kind of collectivism and the other in a free-market economy. The Socialist Party has never managed to put its foot in one camp or another."[7]

With the campaign slogan of "a majority government and a majority president," Sá Carneiro formed a dynamic conservative electoral alliance known as the Democratic Alliance (AD), which joined the PSD, the CDS, and the Popular Monarchist Party (PPM). As the campaign got under way, Sá Carneiro barnstormed the country, emphasizing the themes of tradition, austerity and liberalization. He attacked Soares as an ineffective leader, too complacent in regard to the left-leaning Council of the Revolution. He accused President Eanes of harboring Gaullist ambitions to become the national savior, and of having usurped the powers of the National Assembly.[8] In addition, he committed the Democratic Alliance, if elected, to a revision of the Constitution in order to limit the powers of the President and eliminate the Council of the Revolution.

Although early polls indicated that the AD would win the elections, Sá Carneiro wanted a majority. Given the use of the d'Hondt system of highest averages, he estimated that the AD needed to secure only about 45 percent of the vote in order to receive a majority of seats in the National Assembly. To increase the chances that he would gain a majority, Sá Carneiro promised that if the AD did not receive an absolute majority, he would refuse to form a government, stating to *Expresso:* "I do not want the AD to be a replica of the former Socialist hegemony."[9] Sá Carneiro's gamble was based on his conviction that the people were tired of a weak and ineffective National Assembly, and would choose the AD just to have governmental stability. If the AD failed to secure a majority in 1979, Eanes presumably was going to have Pintasilgo remain as Prime Minister until the 1980 legislative elections.

As the Democratic Alliance started to pick up steam, the left became concerned. Communist Party head Álvaro Cunhal sought to stop the conservative movement by forming a PS-PCP electoral front, but was refused once more by Soares. Instead, the PCP joined forces with the Portuguese Democratic Movement (MDP) in an alliance called the United People's Alliance (APU). In the electoral campaign, the APU employed the latest marketing techniques, and dropped the traditional Communist symbols of the hammer and sickle. If elected, it promised to defend democracy against the rising right.

The Socialists campaigned on the theme of renovation and continuity. Mário Soares condemned the Democratic Alliance and the Communist Party as unacceptable extremists, defended the two years of Socialist rule as pragmatic governance, and positioned the Socialist Party as the vital center between two unreasonable poles. Further, he blamed the parliamentary instability on the persistent presidential interventions.[10]

The National Assembly Elections of 2 December 1979. As shown in Table 3.2, the Democratic Alliance secured a majority in the National Assembly in the 2 December 1979 elections with 42.53 percent of the vote, and 128 of the 250 seats. The Socialists lost some support from the previous legislative elections, winning only 27.33 percent and 74 seats. The Communist-led APU alliance won 18.8 percent of the vote and and 47 seats.

Table 3.2 Results of the National Assembly Elections of 2 December 1979

Party	**APU**	**PS**	**AD**
% of Vote	18.8	27.3	42.53
Seats Won	47	74	128

Note: APU=PCP+MDP; AD=PSD+CDS+PPM. The UDP also won a seat.
Source: *Atlas Eleitoral, 1975–1980* (Lisbon: Editorial Progresso Social e Democracia 1981), 49.

The majority victory of the Democratic Alliance provided the National Assembly with a vigor and legitimacy that had been lacking under Socialist minority rule. The AD's charismatic leader, Francisco Sá Carneiro, had promised great things for his constituency, and there was much anticipation as he assumed the premiership. Conceding defeat, Mário Soares stated that his party's humbling fall had not been "a brilliant performance".[11] Álvaro Cunhal called for leftist unity, noting that the combined total of the APU and the PS was 121 seats. Soares did not rule out voting with the APU on specific measures, but refused to form a common bloc with Cunhal. Municipal elections were held two weeks later.

The 16 December 1979 Municipal Elections. The municipal elections of 16 December confirmed the national conservative trend. The AD scored large victories all over the country, claiming city halls from the Socialist Party in, notably, Lisbon, Faro, Coimbra and Oporto, as evidenced in Table 3.3. After these elections, Prime Minister Maria Pintasilgo handed in her resignation on 27 December 1979. Two days later, President Eanes invited Francisco Sá Carneiro to form a government.[12]

The Sixth Constitutional Government

Keeping to his campaign promises, Sá Carneiro's legislative package included tax cuts, increases in pension payments, a wage freeze, plans to hasten the return of lands to Alentejo plantation owners, and a stop on governmental hiring. He also started the process of amending the Constitution to remove the provisions that protect state control of television and other nationalized industries. The new government is listed in Table 3.4.

Table 3.3 Results of the Municipal Elections of 16 December 1979

Party	APU	PS	AD
% of Vote	17.7	25.5	47.2
City Halls Won	37	115	196
City Councils Won	38	111	54
Local Councils Won	195	1113	1795

Note: APU (PCP+MDP); AD (PSD+CDS+PPM).
Source: Atlas Eleitoral, 1975–1980 (Lisbon: Editorial Progresso Social e Democracia, 1981), 33.

Table 3.4 Composition of the Sixth Constitutional Government

Prime Minister	Francisco Sá Carneiro
Deputy Prime Minister	Freitas do Amaral
Adjunct Prime Minister	Pinto Balsemão
Minister of Foreign Affairs	Freitas do Amaral
Minister of Defense	Amaral da Costa
Minister of Justice	Mário Raposo
Minister of Internal Administration	Eurico de Melo
Minister of Finance and Planning	Cavaco Silva
Minister of Agriculture and Fisheries	Cardoso e Cunha
Minister of Industry and Energy	Ávaro Barreto
Minister of Business and Tourism	Basílio Horta
Minister of Housing and Public Works	João Porta
Minister of Transportation and Communications	Viana Baptista
Minister of Labor	Eusébio de Carvalho
Minister of Social Affairs	Morais Leitão
Minister of Education and Science	Vítor Pereira Crespo

Source: História Contemporânea de Portugal (Lisbon: Amigos do Livro, 1985).

The centerpiece of the AD government was its policy of economic liberalization. Spearheaded by a young economist, Aníbal Cavaco Silva, the government initiated bureaucratic cutbacks, adopted several austerity measures, and liberalized labor laws. Cavaco Silva also opened several previously closed areas of the economy to private investment, including fertilizer, cement, banking, insurance, transports, armaments, oil refining, steel and petrochemical sectors. The only state enterprises that Cavaco Silva did not sell were the unprofitable sectors of electricity, gas, sanitation and transportation. The AD government encouraged foreign investors and provided financial compensations to foreigners who lost properties in the 1974–1976 revolutionary period.[13]

The Council of the Revolution could not stomach these changes. Although for the first three years of constitutional rule, the Council kept out of day-to-day politics, it became much more active and confrontational against the policies of the Democratic Alliance. It did not permit the government to implement the liberalization measures, ruling them unconstitutional.[14]

The 5 October 1980 Legislative Elections. As the regularly scheduled October 1980 legislative elections drew near, the battle lines were clear. The AD had just had a successful year of governing, and was confident of another victory. On the campaign trail, Sá Carneiro promised to revise the Constitution and eliminate the CR in order to implement his liberalization reforms.

The left was under siege from the right, and sought to regain power by instilling the fear of reaction in the people. Promising a return to the center, Mário Soares tried to paint Sá Carneiro as a dangerous extremist. To offset the Democratic Alliance, Soares organized an electoral alliance—called the Republican and Socialist Front (FRS)—with two center-left parties: the Independent Social Democratic Action Party (ASDI) and the Union of the Democratic and Socialist Left (UEDS). Álvaro Cunhal's Communist-led APU campaigned as the true defender of the 25 April revolution, and stated that the AD, representing a serious threat to the Socialist gains of April, had to be stopped.

Sá Carneiro's domestic situation became a campaign issue. He had left his wife without having obtained a divorce, and moved in with a Swedish-born woman, Snub Abacuses. Since he relied on the support of the Catholic and traditional northern and island areas, but was engaged in an adulterous relationship, this was a significant problem. In addition, the left questioned his ethics in other areas. For instance, the Communist newspaper *O Diário* accused Sá Carneiro of a conflict of interest involving the privatization of a state owned bank that had granted him a personal loan.[15]

His personal problems notwithstanding, Sá Carneiro's AD secured an absolute majority in the 5 October 1980 legislative elections. As shown in Table 3.5, the AD overwhelmed the APU and FRS. The center-right AD coalition received 47.1 percent of the vote, and 134 seats. The Socialist-led FRS gained 28 percent of the vote, and 74 seats, and the APU managed to win 16.9 percent of the vote, and 40 seats.

Table 3.5 Results of the National Assembly Elections of 5 October 1980

Party	**APU**	**FRS**	**AD**
% of Vote	16.9	28.0	47.1
Seats Won	40	74	134

Note: APU (PCP+MDP); AD (PSD+CDS+PPM); FRS (PS+UEDS+UDE). The UDP also won a seat.
Source: Atlas Eleitoral, 1975–1980 (Lisbon: Editorial Progresso Social e Democracia, 1981), 49.

Mário Soares acknowledged the electoral defeat, stating that the PS knew how to win elections and how to lose them; a defiant Álvaro Cunhal condemned the AD as a danger to Portuguese democracy.[16] Francisco Sá Carneiro announced in a prepared statement that "the electoral results demonstrate that our political line is the correct one," and promised to the implement AD program.[17] But first, Sá Carneiro turned his attention to finding a candidate who could defeat Ramalho Eanes in the upcoming presidential elections, consistent with the AD's campaign slogan of "one majority government, one majority president."

The 1980 Presidential Election Campaign. After a candidate search, Sá Carneiro announced his support for the conservative General António Soares Carneiro. The general—awkward in public, who is related neither to Mário Soares nor to Francisco Sá Carneiro—was mainly taken seriously because Sá Carnerio wanted him to be President. Prime Minister Sá Carneiro campaigned hard for Soares Carneiro, blaming the political impasse between the government and the Council of the Revolution on President Eanes. He even promised to step down as Prime Minister if Soares Carneiro lost the presidential election. In essence, Soares Carneiro's sole campaign message was that he should be elected to help Sá Carneiro implement the AD program.

In spite of Sá Carneiro's attacks, Eanes remained a popular President. His reelection campaign positioned him as a voice of reason, with the slogan "President for all of the Portuguese." He emphasized the role he had played in maintaining governmental stability, and distanced himself from the military, having stepped down as the head of the military general staff.[18]

Given the threat that Sá Carneiro could completely dominate the political system, Mário Soares agreed to support Eanes' candidacy. With his blessing, the Republican and Socialist Front (FRS) produced campaign commercials for television that featured Eanes and Soares walking, talking and smiling in the gardens at the Belém presidential palace. This anti-Sá Carneiro tactical alliance, however, quickly broke down. At an October news conference, President Eanes, claiming to be in agreement with much of the AD's legislative program, reminded the press that it was he who had dismissed Mário Soares as Prime Minister. Eanes's comment outraged Soares, who demanded that the FRS immediately drop their support for Eanes. Other Socialists, such as Francisco Zenha, asserted that Eanes was merely positioning himself to attract a larger base of support, and that Soares had taken the comment too personally. Arguing that Soares Carnerio represented a far worse danger, the FRS refused Soares' request to withdraw support for Eanes. In protest, Soares resigned as secretary-general of the Socialist Party, splitting it into at least two factions: pro-Soares and pro-Zenha.

There were other candidates in the race as well. The Communist Party nominated Carlos Brito but, fearing the threat of Sá Carneiro, threw its support to Eanes in December. The right-wing general Carlos Galvão de Melo, the dissident leftist Socialist Aires Rodrigues and the right-leaning MFA officer António Pires Veloso also were running. Perhaps most notably, the hero of the 25 April 1974 coup, Otelo Saraiva de Carvalho, sought the presidency as well. When he campaigned for President on a far-left populist program in 1976, thousands of supporters turned out at campaign rallies all over the country. He lost that election to Eanes, but managed a respectable 16.9 percent of the vote. However, in 1980, when he was running on essentially the same political platform, Otelo's campaign rallies were poorly attended. His campaign failure indicated how much Portuguese politics had moderated in just four years.

On 5 December 1980, three days before the scheduled presidential elections, Prime Minister Sá Carneiro and his entourage were killed on their way to an election rally in his hometown of Oporto. Their Cessna C-421 light plane crashed into a home close to Lisbon's Portela airport, soon after it took off. Deputy Prime Minister Diogo Freitas do Amaral immediately assumed Sá Carneiro's duties, and promised a rigorous inquiry into the crash. Supporters have suggested that Sá Carnerio's plane was sabotaged, but no evidence has yet surfaced to prove that a conspiracy existed.[19]

Sá Carneiro's death stunned the nation. President Eanes left a campaign rally to visit the crash site, and was visibly disturbed. Later that day he called off any further campaigning. Sá Carneiro's close associate Francisco Pinto Balsemão stated that in spite of the tragedy, "we have the majority, and will continue to govern."[20] Although the country was in mourning, a multiparty electoral commission ruled that the elections should take place as scheduled.

The 8 December 1980 Presidential Election. Given the death of Sá Carneiro, the presidential election became almost anticlimactic. As indicated in Table 3.6, people clearly voted for the stability of a known leader. Ramalho Eanes easily won his bid for reelection with 56.44 percent of the popular vote, taking the cities of Oporto, Coimbra and Lisbon, as well as the center and southern regions. For his part, Soares Carneiro performed well in the north, some central regions, and in the islands.[21]

Table 3.6 Results of the Presidential Election of 8 December 1980

Candidate	% Vote
António dos Santos Ramalho Eanes	56.44
António Soares Carneiro	40.23
Otelo Saraiva de Carvalho	1.49
Carlos Galvão de Melo	0.84
António Pires Veloso	0.78
Aires Rodrigues	0.22

Source: Atlas Eleitoral, 1975–1980 (Lisbon: Editorial Progresso Social e Democracia, 1981), 44.

The legislative and presidential elections produced somewhat contradictory mandates. The election of the conservative AD was a mandate for change, whereas the reelection of the left-leaning President Eanes was a mandate for stability. These twin and contradictory mandates played out under the governments of the AD. Sá Carneiro's untimely death certainly slowed down the momentum of the AD, but his successor, Francisco Pinto Balsemão, pledged to implement the AD's legislative program.

Perhaps the biggest problem facing Balsemão as he assumed the premiership was the fact that he was not Sá Carneiro. Several AD members could not come to terms with the loss of their leader, and did not accept Balsemão's leadership. Balsemão summed up his dilemma perfectly in an 29 September 1983 interview with the *New York Times*, stating, "It's very difficult to be the successor of a myth."[22]

GOVERNMENTS OF THE DEMOCRATIC ALLIANCE

The Seventh Constitutional Government

Francisco Pinto Balsemão announced the formation of the seventh constitutional government on 4 January 1981. He pledged to govern for the full four-year term, to roll back socialism, and to amend the Constitution. This government is listed in Table 3.7.

The Balsemão government passed a tough austerity package designed to implement the IMF agreement and prepare the country for EEC membership. The short-term consequences of these measures were very bad, as fuel prices and interest rates rapidly increased.[23] In addition, the new administration had to deal with the effects of a five-month drought in the country. The drought strained the economy, forcing the government to make cuts in electricity and limit television broadcasting, and resulted, notably, in low levels of underground water supplies and a 30 percent drop in olive oil production.[24]

Table 3.7 Composition of the Seventh Constitutional Government

Prime Minister	Pinto Balsemão
Adjunct Prime Minister	Basílio Horta
Minister of Foreign Affairs	Gonçalves Pereira
Minister of Defense	Azevedo Coutinho
Minister of Justice	Meneres Pimentel
Minister of Internal Administration	Monteiro do Amaral
Minister of Finance and Planning	Morais Leitão
Minister of Agriculture and Fisheries	Cardoso e Cunha
Minister of Industry and Energy	Bayão Horta
Minister of Business and Tourism	Alexandre Vaz Pinto
Minister of Housing and Public Works	Luis Barbosa
Minister of Transportation and Communications	Viana Baptista
Minister of Labor	Nascimento Rodriques
Minister of Social Affairs	Carlos Macedo
Minister of Education and Science	Vítor Pereira Crespo
Minister of Quality of Life	Freitas do Amaral
Minister of European Intergration	Álvaro Barreto

Source: História Contemporânea de Portugal (Lisbon: Amigos do Livro, 1985).

Throughout the period the Communist-dominated unions resisted the AD government, and called strikes in protest of the austerity measures in a number of sectors, including railroads, postal service, and phone service.[25] This wave of strikes eroded Balsemão's authority, and led several AD coalition partners to criticize his leadership skills. CDS ministers Diogo do Amaral and Basílio Horta, among others, claimed that he was too willing to be conciliatory to his opponents. As the economic situation and social turmoil worsened, Carlos Macedo, PSD Minister of Social Affairs, resigned on 27 July 1981 to protest Balsemão's leadership style. In response to his critics, Balsemão announced on 10 August 1981 that he intended to resign. President Eanes accepted his resignation the next day, and asked the AD to suggest a new candidate for Prime Minister.[26]

Balsemão's critics failed to present a replacement candidate, leaving Eanes no option other than to invite Balsemão to form a new government on 18 August 1981. In retrospect, it is quite clear that Balsemão's decision to resign was merely a ploy to silence his critics. He had reasoned that there were no other suitable candidates, and wanted the constant criticism from his own AD coalition to stop. Like it or not, the AD was stuck with Balsemão.

The Eighth Constitutional Government

Having outmaneuvered his critics, Balsemão formed a new government, listed in Table 3.8, and turned his attention to the economic and military challenges facing the regime. To address the economic challenge, Balsemão proposed a three-year austerity program aimed at reviving the economy and bringing Portugal into the EEC. This program sought to improve exports and reduce the country's dependency on food imports. He also wanted to reduce the inflation rate.[27] The key achievement of Balsemão's administration, however, was his masterful handling of the military challenge. The Council of the Revolution (CR), which had vetoed over forty AD legislative bills, remained "a source of constant irritation for the center and right."[28] To eliminate the CR, Balsemão needed to gain the support of the Socialist Party to pass a constitutional revision. The AD-PS combined seats represented 208 of the 250 total seats in the National Assembly, which would easily meet the Constitution's two-thirds requirement for revision.

After a divisive internal battle, Mário Soares was reelected as the Socialist Party's general secretary in 1981. A short while later, Balsemão approached Soares about his plans for a constitutional revision, appealing both to Soares' commitment to democracy, and to his resentment of presidential interference into the affairs of the National Assembly. Glad to be back in the thick of things, Soares was willing to work out a deal with the AD.

The 1982 Constitutional Revision. The terms of the negotiated Balsemão-Soares constitutional revision led to a shift of institutional power away from the President and to the National Assembly. It reduced the President's powers regarding the dismissal of a Prime Minister, eliminated the Council of the Revolution and modified the Socialist provisions to allow for private investment in certain nationalized sectors. In the place of the Council of the Revolution, the revision created a Constitutional Court, whose members are elected by the National Assembly and which is responsible to judge the constitutionality of laws.[29] In a concession to Soares, the revisions did not remove the language committing Portugal to socialism. This revision passed the National Assembly with the support of the AD and PS deputies.

The AD-PS also agreed to the terms of a new Defense Law, which made the President's role as Commander in Chief merely symbolic, ensured that the senior governmental official in charge of defense would be the Defense Minister and that the heads of the general staffs of the armed services would be selected by the Prime Minister. President Eanes vetoed this bill, but the National Assembly overrode his veto.[30]

Table 3.8 Composition of the Eighth Constitutional Government

Prime Minister	Pinto Balsemão
Deputy Prime Minister	Freitas do Amaral
Adjunct Prime Minister	Monteiro do Amaral
Minister of Foreign Affairs	Gonçalves Pereira
Minister of Defense	Freitas do Amaral
Minister of Justice	Meneres Pimentel
Minister of Internal Administration	Angelo Correira
Minister of Agriculture, Commerce and Fisheries	Basílio Horta
Minister of Industry and Energy	Bayão Horta
Minister of Business and Tourism	João Salgueiro
Minister of Housing and Public Works	Viana Baptista
Minister of Transportation and Communications	Alexandre Vaz Pinto
Minister of Labor	Queiros Martins
Minister of Social Affairs	Luis Barbosa
Minister of Education and Science	Vítor Pereira Crespo
Minister of Quality of Life	Ribeiro Teles
Minister of Culture and Scientific Coordination	Lucas Pires

Source: História Contemporânea de Portugal (Lisbon: Amigos do Livro, 1985).

The End of Military Involvement in Politics. The members of the Council of the Revolution did not agree with the constitutional revision nor with the conservative politics of the Democratic Alliance. However, the revisions were carried out in accordance with the Constitution, and, as such, were binding on the CR. Accepting the legitimacy of the democratic process—even while opposing the content of the decision—council members submitted their resignations.[31] The CR officially disbanded in a ceremony on 28 October 1982, and President Eanes saluted their role in the democratic transition:

> Today we can affirm with pride that our promises made as members of the armed forces concerning Portuguese democracy have been fulfilled . . . the transfer of politico-military powers to legitimate elected institutions has taken place as we promised the Portuguese. With the constitutional revision in force the armed forces assumes its normal place in a democracy.[32]

The significance of the 1982 constitutional revision was twofold. First, it eliminated the role of the military in the political process. Second, it paved the way for three political parties (PS, PSD, CDS) that shared different ideologies to cooperate closely for the sake of civilian and parliamentary rule.[33] Only the Communist Party voted against the revision. As a result of the revision, the National Assembly became stronger as an institution, which advanced the consolidation.[34]

The Unraveling of the Democratic Alliance

Balsemão was a competent Prime Minister, but two turbulent years of governing had eroded some of the AD's support among civil sectors. In particular, in spite of the austerity measures the economy showed few signs of improvement.[35] In its annual review of the Portuguese economy, the OECD noted that Portugal continued to suffer from large government deficits and a permissive credit system.[36] It was the disappointing performance in the 1982 municipal elections, however, that finished the Democratic Alliance.

The AD actually won these elections, gaining 42 percent of the total vote. The problem was that since its total was down by 7 percent from the last municipal elections in 1979, the outcome was widely interpreted as a rejection of AD rule. Mário Soares' rejuvenated Socialist Party won 30 percent of the vote, and recaptured the city councils in Lisbon, Coimbra and Oporto. The Communist Party won 20 percent, and gained five town halls.

Taking these results as a vote of no confidence, Prime Minister Balsemão resigned and suggested that the head of the PSD parliamentary group, Vítor Crespo, take over as Prime Minister. When Balsemão's Democratic Alliance partner, Diogo Freitas do Amaral, rejected Crespo as Prime Minister, President Eanes ordered interim elections for 25 April 1983—the ninth anniversary of the coup. Eanes justified his decision on the grounds that the Democratic Alliance's internal divisions were hindering governmental stability. Portugal again turned to elections to resolve a governmental crisis.[37]

The 1983 Legislative Campaign

The official three-week campaign got under way on 4 April, launched by the blanketing of Portuguese cities and towns with campaign posters by various political activists. The campaign ran very smoothly, and early polls indicated that Mário Soares and the Socialist Party would win.[38] With the collapse of the Democratic Alliance, the right was in general disarray, and the left sensed an opportunity to regain the National Assembly.

The PSD was under the leadership of former Prime Minister Carlos Mota Pinto. Known as a competent technocrat, he did not radiate much charisma, and failed to define a campaign message other than that the PS was not trustworthy.

Mota Pinto was in the unenviable position of distancing the PSD from Prime Minister Pinto Balsemão. He needed to place the blame for the bad economic situation on Balsemão personally, not on the PSD.

Thirty-eight-year-old Francisco Lucas Pires headed the CDS list, and claimed to be the true heir of the Democratic Alliance. He blamed former Prime Minister Balsemão for being too soft on the Socialists and President Eanes. In the tradition of Sá Carneiro, the CDS promised to direct an aggressive, anti-left government.

The Socialist Party was led by a revitalized Mário Soares, who focused the electoral campaign on the poor state of the economy. If elected, he promised to tackle the economic mess with "100 measures in the first 100 days" of his administration. Soares also pledged that, in contrast to 1976, he would not lead a minority government. Emphasizing moderate themes, he argued that short-term sacrifice was necessary for economic recovery. This campaign highlighted Soares's well known international contacts, asking the people if there were any candidate better equipped to represent Portugal as it prepared to enter the EEC.

The Communist Party, guided by Álvaro Cunhal, returned to its familiar theme as the party of the 25 April 1974 revolution. The PC, running once more as the APU, promised to roll back the privatizations carried out by the Democratic Alliance, and to place Portugal back on the road to socialism.

The Elections of 25 April 1983. Taking advantage of the breakdown of the Democratic Alliance and the popularity of Mário Soares, the Socialist Party won the elections with 36.12 percent of the vote, its highest percentage in nine years. The PSD came in second with 29.87 percent of the vote, and the CDS received 9.96 percent. The APU improved slightly from its 1980 vote total, gaining 18.07 percent.[39] These results are shown in Table 3.9.

Table 3.9 Results of the National Assembly Elections of 25 April 1983

Party	APU	PS	PSD	CDS
% of Vote	18.07	36.12	29.87	9.96
Seats Won	44	101	88	22

Note: APU= PCP+MDP.
Source: Manuel Braga da Cruz and Miguel Lobo Antunes, "Revolutionary Transition and Problems of Parliamentary Institutionalization: The Case of the Portuguese National Assembly," in Ulrike Liebert and Maurizio Cotto, eds., *Parliament and Democratic Consolidation in Southern Europe* (London: Pinter, 1990), 163.

Soares approached the PSD about forming a majority government, maintaining that the two parties presented moderate programs and represented over 60 percent of the vote.[40] Mota Pinto accepted Soares' invitation, and a new governing experiment, known as the Central Bloc, got under way. President Eanes was only too happy to accept this arrangement, which he had suggested several times during the 1976–1978 period.

CONCLUSION

This second period was characterized by an assertive National Assembly confronting the military challenge. The elimination of the Council of the Revolution demonstrated that a purposeful and unified political alliance in the National Assembly could dominate the other actors in the political system. This experience convinced many political actors that a successful consolidation of the regime was indeed possible.

NOTES

1. Diogo Freitas do Amaral, "The Constitution and Governance in Portugal," in Kenneth R. Maxwell and Scott C. Monge, eds., *The Constitution and the Consolidation of Democracy, 1976–1989* (New York: Camões Center, Columbia University, 1991), 8.

2. *Expresso*, 21 July 1979.

3. See 28 July 1979 *Expresso*. *Expresso Revista*, 4 August 1979, has a story on her cabinet.

4. See *Expresso Revista*, 21 July 1979.

5. Interview with Maria de Lourdes Pintasilgo, *Diário de Notícias*, 3 January 1980.

6. *Expresso Revista*, 31 March 1979, provides a very good analysis of the political situation.

7. *New York Times*, 29 July 1979.

8. See the political analysis by José António Saraiva, *"Eanes-Presidente-Rei sem Presidentialismo," Expresso*, 28 July 1979. Saraiva offers a critique of Eanes' political decisions and interventions.

9. *Expresso*, 31 January 1979.

10. *Expresso Revista, 11 August 1979,* features a series on the parties preparing for the elections, including slogans and strategies: "Partidos Preparam Eleições: Que Alianças? Que Listas?"

11. *Le Monde*, 4 December 1979.

12. See Marcelo Rebelo de Sousa, *"O Isolamento Crescente de Maria de Lourdes Pintasilgo," Expresso,* 8 September 1979 on the growing isolation of Pintasilgo.

13. Cavaco Silva, part of a new generation of Portuguese leaders, earned his doctorate in economics at the University of York in England. He had very little to do with the revolutionary period. See Martin Kayman, *Revolution and Counterrevolution in Portugal* (London: Merlin Press, 1987), 215.

14. See Walter C. Opello, *Portugal: From Monarchy to Pluralist Democracy* (Boulder: Westview Press, 1991) 107–109; Kayman, 214.

15. See *O Diário*, various issues in September and October 1979, in which Sá Carneiro's character is attacked.

16. See reports in *Diário de Notícias*, 6 October 1980.

17. Francisco Sá Carneiro, *Textos Vol. 6* (Lisbon: Editorial Progresso Social e Democracia, 1990), 423.

18. Lawrence S. Graham, *The Portuguese Military and the State* (Boulder, CO: Westview Press, 1993), 3.

19. Also killed were Snub Abacuses, Defense Minister Adelino Amaral da Costa and his wife; António Patrício Gouveia, an aide; and the two pilots. *Diário de Notícias,* 6 December 1980.

20. *New York Times*, 8 December 1980.

21. *Diário de Notícias*, 9 December 1980.

22. Balsemão, speaking of Sá Carneiro, in *New York Times*, 29 January 1983.

23. *Wall Street Journal*, 20 July 1981.

24. Ibid., 19 February 1981.

25. Ibid., 5 March 1981.

26. See reports in *Diário de Notícias*, especially 11 August 1981.

27. Ibid., 20 August 1981.

28. Graham, 48

29. António Vitorino, "The Politics of Constitutional Revision," in Kenneth R. Maxwell and Scott C. Monje, eds., *Portugal: The Constitution and the Consolidation of Democracy, 1976–1989* (New York: Camões Center, Columbia University, 1991) 17–22.

30. Graham, 49.

31. See discussion in ibid., 34–39.

32. *Diário de Notícias*, 29 October 1982; the text of the new constitution is printed in *Diário de Notícias*, 27 August 1982.

33. See Graham, 82–88.

34. The Council of the Revolution officers formed a new group, called the *Association of 25 April.* At first, many wondered if it would lead to another military coup, but it has developed into a retired officers' club.

35. The inflation rate was 22.5 percent in December 1982. *Wall Street Journal*, 1 December 1982.

36. *OECD, Report on Portugal* (Washington, D.C.: Organization for Economic Cooperation and Development, 1982), 1.

37. *Expresso*, 20 November 1982; *O Dia*, 23 January 1983; *Diário de Noticias*, 23 January 1983.

38. *Expresso*, April 1983.

39. See *Expresso*, 7 May 1983; Jorge Gaspar and Nuno Vitorino, *As Eleições de 25 de Abril-Geografia e Imagem dos Partidos* (Lisbon: Livros Horizonte, 1976); David Goldey, "Elections and the Consolidation of Portuguese Democracy, 1974–1983" *Electoral Studies* 2, no. 3, (1983):229–240.

40. Eusébio Mujal-León, "The Portuguese Elections of 1983: The Portuguese Party System in Flux," Unpublished Manuscript, 1984.

4

The Consolidation's Third Period: The National Assembly Realizes Political Stability and Economic Growth, 1983–1991

Starting in 1983, the PS-PSD government, known as the Central Bloc, implemented a series of economic reforms which were deepened and enhanced by the PSD governments after 1985. In addition, the election of a PSD legislative majority in 1987 and 1991 furthered governmental stability. This chapter examines the consolidation's third and final period, characterized by a dominant National Assembly effectively confronting its economic and political challenges.

THE CENTRAL BLOC GOVERNMENT

The Ninth Constitutional Government

Based on the PS-PSD agreement, Mário Soares named PSD head Mota Pinto to be his Deputy Prime Minister, and proposed a center-right economic plan, in line with the IMF economic stabilization program.[1] This government, listed in Table 4.1, was easily passed by the National Assembly.

Soares' Economic Agenda. To promote state solvency and economic competitiveness, Soares pledged 10 percent of the national gold reserves to guarantee governmental loans, ordered the devaluation of the escudo by 12 percent to improve Portugal's export position and lowered governmental subsidies.[2] In addition, the National Assembly passed legislation on 6 July 1983 permitting private enterprise in the banking, insurance, cement, and fertilizer industries. Other measures allowed businessmen to lay off workers. Similar bills had been passed by the Democratic Alliance, only to be vetoed by the Council of the Revolution.

Table 4.1 Composition of the Ninth Constitutional Government

Prime Minister	Mário Soares
Deputy Prime Minister	Mota Pinto
Minister of Foreign Affairs	Jaime Gama
Minister of Defense	Mota Pinto
Minister of Justice	Rui Machete
Minister of Internal Administration	Eduardo Pereira
Minister of Finance	Ermani Lopes
Minister of Agriculture and Fisheries	Manuel Soares da Costa
Minister of Industry and Technology	João Veiga Simão
Minister of Labor	Amandio de Azevedo
Minister of Social Affairs	José Rosado Correira

Source: História Contemporânea de Portugal (Lisbon: Amigos do Livro, 1985).

The government turned to the IMF for assistance, and agreed to a letter of intent on 19 October 1983, promising, among other measures, to hold down wages for civil servants and limit hiring. Soares also reduced subsidies on sugar, wheat, milk, codfish, fuel, electricity and postage. He justified these actions as necessary for the national economy, and called on workers to make sacrifices to attain economic stability.[3] Communist union activists rejected Soares' calls for moderation, and organized several national strikes in June and July. Strikes disrupted bus and subway systems in Lisbon during the summer of 1983.[4]

The Popular Forces of 25 April (FP-25). The turn to the right by the Socialist Party confirmed the worst fear of the far left: that the people had been duped by the Socialist Party. In their view, Soares had not only permitted a complete recovery of the right, he was actually leading the way. One far-left faction, called the Popular Forces of April 25 (FP-25), which lamented the loss of the 25 April 1974 revolution to the bourgeois, decided to take up arms against the democratic regime. The FP-25 was linked to the hero of the 25 April 1974 revolution, Otelo Saraiva de Carvalho, who had become distressed with the recovery of the right. In response to the Democratic Alliance, he formed a far-left-wing political party known as the Popular Unity Force (FUP) in 1980 to back his presidential bid. Government officials became suspicious that the FUP was political front for a terrorist group when the FP-25 was organized later that year. Otelo has always denied involvement with the FP-25, although he has admitted that "the ideological convictions of the militants are very similar to mine. They are men who sincerely fight for an ideal."[5]

Throughout the 1980s, the FP-25 engaged in a low-intensity national terrorist campaign of bombings, bank robberies and killings. Among others, they killed industrialists and company administrators. To commemorate the ninth anniversary of the failed 25 November 1975 left-wing coup attempt, FP-25 terrorists attacked the American Embassy with grenades, causing some damage but killing no one. They also launched grenades from the coastline against NATO ships.[6] On 20 June 1984, Portuguese police raided several locations of the FP-25 in Lisbon, and arrested over seventy people. These raids uncovered explosives, guns and money. The police also arrested Otelo, and charged him with heading a terrorist organization.

In October 1985, in what was described as Portugal's "trial of the century," Otelo was charged with secretly leading a band of extreme leftist terrorists in an attempt to undermine the regime. Nineteen months and five hundred witnesses later, a three judge panel found Otelo guilty, and sentenced him to fifteen years in prison. Forty-seven co-defendants were found guilty, and sixteen were acquitted.[7]

This challenge to political stability was taken very seriously by Mário Soares. His government submitted tough anti-terrorist legislation to crack down on the activities of the FP-25, passed by the National Assembly. The legislation allowed police to tap telephones and open mail without obtaining a search warrant. Although this legislation was reminiscent of the Salazar/Caetano period, Soares stated that it was essential to combat terrorism and organized crime.

The End of the Central Bloc

The two years of the Central Bloc governance were good ones for the young regime. Political bickering was at a minimum, the institutional relationship between Eanes and Soares was good, the government improved the economic situation, and Portugal prepared to enter the European Economic Community (EEC). The 1986 OEDC economic survey of Portugal noted the improvements:

> The economic situation of Portugal in 1986 is appreciably better than at the time of the last survey (the first half of 1984). A current payment deficit of $3.2 billion in 1982 (around 13 per cent of GDP) had led to the introduction of a strict austerity policy in 1983. The deficit has been gradually reduced and 1985 saw even a surplus. While the improvement in the external account was achieved in part through a decline in purchasing power and domestic demand, the unemployment consequences remained limited. On the inflation front, the annual rate of increase in retail prices was reduced from almost 30 per cent in mid-1984 to close to 17 per cent at the end of 1985.[8]

Portugal's membership in the EEC was a crowning achievement for the new democracy. With the approval of the National Assembly, Prime Minister Soares signed the treaty of adherence to the EEC on 12 June 1985, to take effect on 1 January 1986. Only the Communist deputies opposed the treaty. A 15 June 1985 *Expresso* editorial praised the EEC treaty, stating that it was a tribute to the new democracy. The editorial also pointed out that in spite of their political and ideological differences, all of the Prime Ministers since 1976 had worked toward the goal of EEC membership. In addition, it asserted that this step would help Portugal modernize and, in due course, achieve the high living standards of the other EEC member countries.[9] The signing of the treaty caused a momentary political pause in Portugal as the PS, PSD and CDS celebrated the achievement. After a few days of celebration, political life returned to normal, and the parties prepared for another round of legislative and presidential elections.

Given its economic successes, the collapse of the Central Bloc government was not brought about by internal divisions but by Soares' personal ambition. In a thinly disguised effort to leave his position in order to prepare for the upcoming presidential elections, he offered to resign on 13 June 1985 over a minor PS-PSD disagreement regarding economic issues. Soares' PSD coalition partners denied that there was any real disagreement, stating that the only problem was that Soares wanted to delay some further austerity measures to improve his popularity and electoral chances.[10] Given Soares' determination to resign as Prime Minister, President Eanes agreed to his demands on the condition that the current government stay in place until the National Assembly approved the final version of the treaty of accession to the European Economic Community (EEC). The President stated that legislative interim elections would take place on 6 October 1985.

The 1985 National Assembly Electoral Campaign

A new political party, the Democratic Renewal Party (PRD)—formed as a vehicle for outgoing President Eanes to stay involved in politics—participated in the 1985 campaign. Since the Constitution prohibited Eanes from running for a third consecutive term, and from campaigning for another office while he was President, Eanes' wife, Manuela, actually founded the PRD with Hermínio Martins. The PRD's political program openly invoked the President's name, proposing that this moderate, pragmatic and leftist party could renew Portuguese democracy. The PRD had the advantages of representing a popular President and having absolutely no responsibility for the economic situation or previous austerity measures.

Four other significant parties competed. The Socialist Party campaigned without Mário Soares, who was preparing for his Presidential bid. The PS, led by António de Almeida Santos, argued that it had helped Portugal face its economic difficulties, but the continuing adverse affects of Soares' austerity measures hurt the PS's overall chances. The PSD was led by Aníbal Cavaco Silva, who positioned himself as a follower of Sá Carneiro. Cavaco Silva, a tenured professor of economics at Catholic University in Lisbon, blamed the Socialist Party for the economic crisis and promised to implement liberalization policies to improve the economic situation. On the far-right, the CDS promised a conservative legislative package, including rapid denationalizations of state-owned businesses; on the far-left, the PCP promised to undo the liberalization policies adopted by the Democratic Alliance and the Central Bloc.

The National Assembly Elections of 8 October 1985. As indicated in Table 4.2, the PSD emerged as the winner of these elections, gaining 29.87 percent of the vote, nine percentage points higher than the PS. The PRD came in third with a surprising 17.97 percent total. The PCP and CDS totals were down: receiving 15.5 percent and 9.96 percent respectively.

Table 4.2 Results of the National Assembly Elections of 8 October 1985

Party	PCP	PS	PRD	PSD	CDS
% of Vote	15.5	20.77	17.97	29.87	9.96
Seats Won	39	57	45	88	22

Note: The remaining 5.93 percent was divided among smaller parties.
Source: Facts on File World News Digest, 24 July 1987, 538D1.

Formed only a few months before the election, the PRD, along with the PSD and PS, had suddenly become a major player in legislative politics. Its leader, Hermínio Martins, said that he was unwilling to join a coalition but would support a minority government in the National Assembly if it would commit to implementing the PRD's campaign pledges of loyal cooperation with President Eanes, fairer distribution of wealth, and payment of backwages owed to state workers. Cavaco Silva agreed to these terms, and formed the tenth constitutional government.

THE PSD GOVERNMENTS

The Tenth Constitutional Government

Cavaco Silva pledged that his minority PSD government, listed in Table 4.3, would liberalize the economy. Unlike Soares' minority PS governments in the late 1970s, Cavaco's minority government took power during an advantageous economic time. In particular, Portugal officially joined the EEC on 1 January

1986, which helped to stabilize the economic situation. As Cavaco started to govern, national attention turned to the presidential election.

Table 4.3 Composition of the Tenth Constitutional Government

Prime Minister	Aníbal Cavaco Silva
Deputy Prime Minister	Eurico de Melo
Minister of Foreign Affairs	João de Deus Pinheiro
Minister of Defense	Eurico de Melo
Minister of Justice	Fernando Nogueira
Minister of Internal Administration	José Silveira Godinho
Minister of Finance	Miguel Cadilhe
Minister of Agriculture and Fisheries	Álvaro Barreto
Minister of Industry and Energy	Luis Mira Amaral
Minister of Parliamentary Affairs	António Capucho
Minister of Portuguese Overseas Communities	Corresa Neves
Minister of Foreign Business	Durão Barrosa
Minister of Culture	Teresa Gouveia

Source: Jornal do Comercial, 1 January 1987.

The 1986 Presidential Election

The presidential election of 1986 was extremely important for at least two reasons. First, it was the first presidential election since 1976 without an important military candidate, and second, it would indicate the overall direction and tone of the regime. Four major candidates competed.

On the right, the CDS and PSD were united in their support of CDS head Diogo Freitas do Amaral. If elected, he promised to pursue a conservative agenda with the PSD government. Among other measures, he promised to help with the liberalization of the economy and to implement educational reforms. Further, Amaral contended that a conservative president was the best way to gain the confidence of business and foreign investors.[11]

The left was divided among several prominent candidates. Socialist Mário Soares campaigned on the themes of stability and moderation. Former Prime Minister Maria de Lourdes Pintasilgo ran as a Socialist independent, promising to alleviate the suffering of workers. Francisco Salgado Zenha, who had battled Soares over the party's support for Eanes in 1980, ran as a Socialist alternative to Soares. Zenha was supported by the PCP and by outgoing President Eanes and the PRD.[12]

In the first round of voting, on 6 February 1986, Freitas do Amaral routed his leftist opponents with 47 percent of the vote, just 3.1 percent shy of an outright victory. Soares came in second place with 25 percent of the vote, Zenha received 21 percent and Pintasilgo won 7 percent. This was a particularly bad outcome for the left. Amaral was arguably one of the most right-wing politicians in Portugal, and the CDS included some of the most conservative elements of society. For their part, the CDS was thrilled—their candidate only needed to convince 3.1 percent more of the electorate to vote for him, and the CDS would control the presidency.

Under the electoral rules of Portugal, if no candidate captures a majority in the first round of voting, a second round takes place between the two top vote getters. Fortunately for the left, the candidate who advanced to the second round against Amaral was Soares. A very adept and cagy politician, Soares always seemed to come alive in impossible situations, as he had done in the anticommunist struggles of 1975. He understood that a good campaign, along with pragmatic, tactical anti-Amaral voting, could enable him to win the presidency.

In the second round of campaigning, Amaral continued with his themes of reform and liberalization, and contended that a CDS President and a PSD Prime Minister could accomplish an economic miracle. Soares campaigned less on a specific set of proposals and more on his leadership skills. He projected an image as a consensus maker and as the candidate able to unite all of the Portuguese. Soares argued that since Portugal already had a conservative Prime Minister, a center-left President was necessary to balance the system and prevent any governmental excesses.

Expresso focused on the presidential elections in its 14 February 1986 edition, asking a number of former government leaders for whom they were voting. The head of the first provisional government, Adelino da Palma Carlos, stated that he would vote for Freitas do Amaral, describing him as "the person who best brings together the necessary conditions" for the presidency.[13] Former presidential candidate Pintasilgo supported Mário Soares. She believed that Soares could unify the people and deliver political stability.

Perhaps the most typical expression of the calculations of the left was stated by former Prime Minister Vasco Gonçalves, the pro-Communist MFA officer who had led the second, third, fourth and fifth provisional governments. Gonçalves considered Soares a lesser evil than Amaral, whose victory would start a "fascist dynamic." Consequently, Gonçalves planned "to vote against Freitas do Amaral."[14]

With a united left supporting him, Soares defeated Amaral in the 16 February 1986 voting with 51 percent of the vote. Soares was also supported by some centrist and center-right elements, who felt that Portugal was not ready for an extreme right-wing President. Soares was known to be an able negotiator and a pragmatist. Further, voters believed that his connections would help Portugal regain a positive international image.[15] In fact, a number of notable foreign leaders attended Soares' 9 March 1986 inauguration as President. Present were President François Mitterand of France, Prime Minister Felipe Gonzalez of Spain, and Vice President George Bush of the United States. In his inaugural address, Soares took note of their presence, stating that Portugal's new democracy had ended the country's long isolation, and had earned the respect of the world's leading nations.[16]

An Improving Economy. President Soares and Prime Minister Cavaco Silva developed a good working relationship. Soares stayed out of day-to-day politics, emphasizing his conciliatory role. In addition, Cavaco's economic policies, helped by EEC funds, had generated some very positive signs. EEC investment helped stabilize the domestic market, making it much more attractive to foreign investors. In addition, falling world oil prices and a weak American dollar contributed to the recovery. Combined, these factors helped Portugal experience a 4 percent economic growth in 1986, and brought its inflation rate down to 12 percent from 20 percent the year before. Direct foreign investment in Portugal jumped 152 percent in 1987.[17]

The Collapse of the PSD Minority Government. In spite of the positive economic performance, the PRD introduced a censure motion against Cavaco on 3 April 1987, forcing the collapse of the minority government. Apparently the PRD had hoped to convince the PS to support former President Eanes as the new Prime Minister. The PS, led by Vítor Constâncio, refused to cooperate with the PRD, arguing that the new Prime Minister should be a Socialist. In the absence of viable alternatives, President Soares called for new elections for the National Assembly.[18]

Cavaco's PSD welcomed Soares' decision. On 4 April 1987, *Expresso* had published a poll indicating that the PSD could capture an outright absolute majority, and the PSD felt that it had governed well since 1985.[19] Its campaign slogan, "Portugal cannot stop," warned that all of the good economic progress could return to chaos if the PSD did not gain an absolute victory.

Vítor Constâncio positioned the Socialist Party as the center-left alternative to the PSD, and as the only moderate party that could deal with the economic problems as well as be compassionate. The Socialists warned that the PSD would implement harsh austerity measures, and contended that a legislative Socialist majority would complement the Socialist President.[20] The basis of the PRD campaign was that if the party achieved a majority, it would propose former President Eanes as Prime Minister. Its 1985 legislative success was linked to the popularity of Eanes, but since he had been out of office for almost two years, there were questions as to whether he could still attract votes.

On the far-left, the PCP allied itself with the MDP under the CDU banner. It invoked the hopes of 25 April, and promised to stop the recovery of the right. On the far-right, the success of the center-right PSD was causing problems for the CDS. Now led by Adriano Moreira, the CDS did not offer a conservative vision distinct from that of the PSD, and it had seen its support drop off in the last few elections. Amaral's close loss in the 1986 presidential election had certainly demoralized the party, and the CDS ran a lackluster campaign.

The National Assembly Elections of 19 July 1987. The National Assembly elections of 19 July 1987 were a watershed event for the consolidation of the regime. As shown in Table 4.4, the PSD gained an absolute majority with 50.15 percent of the vote. This victory provided the regime with an extended period of political stability, and was widely interpreted as a positive judgment of Cavaco's leadership of the PSD minority government since 1985. He had capably streamlined the Portuguese bureaucracy and overseen Portugal's successful entry into the EEC.

Table 4.4 Results of the National Assembly Elections of 19 July 1987

Party	CDU	PS	PRD	PSD	CDS
% of Vote	12.18	22.32	4.93	50.15	4.34
Seats Won	20	59	7	146	4

Note: CDU=PCP+MDP+Greens. The remaining 6.08 percent was divided among smaller parties.
Source: Manuel Braga da Cruz and Miguel Lobo Antunes, "Revolutionary Transition and Problems of Parliamentary Institutionalization: The Case of the Portuguese National Assembly," in Ulrike Liebert and Maurizio Cotto, eds., *Parliament and Democratic Consolidation in Southern Europe* (London: Pinter, 1990), 163.

With 22.32 percent of the vote, the PS emerged as the leading opposition party. Indeed, given the PSD's absolute victory, the PS was consoled in that it had slightly improved its electoral margin from 1985. With a Socialist President, and as the clear leader of the opposition, the PS was in fair political shape.

The Communists continued their electoral slide downward, receiving 12.18 percent of the total. Álvaro Cunhal's rhetoric about defending the gains of 25 April continued to have some appeal in the Alentejo, but was rejected by most of the nation. The PCP seemed to be in a process of irreversible decline, even suffering losses in its strongholds of Beja, Setúbal, Évora, and Portalegre. After the 1987 elections, the Communists were very concerned about the future viability of their party.[21]

For the CDS, too, the absolute victory of the PSD was not a good outcome. CDS leader Adriano Moreira lost any leverage he might have had if the PSD had failed to achieve 50 percent of the total vote. In addition, the CDS only received 4.44 percent of the vote, meaning that many of its supporters had voted for the PSD.

The biggest losers of the elections were the PRD and former President Ramalho Eanes. The PRD had badly timed the censure motion against Cavaco, and its 4.93 percent vote total was a clear rejection of Eanes. The PRD had been a political vehicle for the former President, and this defeat left the party without a clear purpose. Eanes resigned from his PRD leadership position in August.[22]

José António Saraiva has correctly observed that this election was less a left-right ideological struggle than a vote for political stability. In his view, the rejection of Amaral in the 1986 presidential election paralleled the 1987 National Assembly elections: just as a vote for Amaral was a vote for an unknown commodity, a vote for the left in the legislative elections was a vote for the unknown as well. On the other hand, both Soares of the PS and Cavaco Silva of the PSD were known quantities. That is, the country voted for Cavaco in 1987 for essentially the same reasons it voted for Soares in 1986: each candidate was able to transmit the qualities of competence, stability and security to the electorate.[23]

The Eleventh Constitutional Government

Cavaco Silva committed his government to liberalizing the economy. His four-year economic plan sought to achieve the twin goals of reducing state involvement and increasing private investment in the economy. He planned to sell state-owned companies, ease labor laws and encourage entrepreneurial activity.[24] On 13 August 1987, Cavaco Silva presented his new cabinet, which is listed in Table 4.5.

The 1989 constitutional revision. By 1988, Cavaco sensed that the time was right for another constitutional revision, and approached PS head Vítor Constâncio about his proposed changes. Specifically, he sought to delete the provision that committed Portugal to the creation of a socialist state. Constâncio agreed with Cavaco, for he himself had earlier convinced the Socialist Party to delete all references to Marxism in the party statement. This constitutional revision replaced the wording of the Constitution that pledged the government to the creation of a "classless society" with the new goal of "trying to construct a free, just and united society."[25] On 1 June 1989 the Portuguese National Assembly, with the dissent of the Communist Party, overwhelmingly approved the constitutional revision.

Economic Recovery. Spurred by a combination of Cavaco's economic policies and membership in the EEC, Portugal enjoyed the fastest growth rate in Europe from 1987 to 1991: a yearly average of 4.5 percent growth. The government liberalization program included the sale of public shares equal to 49 percent of Banco Português do Atlântico and Banco Totta e Açores, and also partially privatized the Unicer brewery.[26] As indicated in Table 4.6, the economy's main macroeconomic indicators demonstrated this rapid growth.

Table 4.5 Composition of the Eleventh Constitutional Government

Prime Minister	Aníbal Cavaco Silva
Minister of the Presidency	Fernando Nogueira
Minister of Foreign Affairs	João de Deus Pinheiro
Minister of Defense	Fernando Nogueira
Minister of Justice	Laborinho Lucio
Minister of Internal Administration	Manuel Pereira
Minister of Finance	Miguel Beleza
Minister of Education	Roberto Caneiro
Minister of Agriculture and Fisheries	Arlindo Cunha
Minister of Industry and Energy	Luis Mira Amaral
Minister of Parliamentary Affairs	Dias Loureiro
Minister of Public Works	Joaquim Martins Ferreira do Amaral

Source: Jornal do Comercial, 14 August 1987.

The EEC and Portugal. The EEC played a large role in the economic recovery, having assumed the responsibility of gradually raising Portugal's living standard to that of other European countries as of 1 January 1986. By 1991, the EEC had invested over five billion US dollars in Portugal for the construction of new roads, including a Lisbon-Oporto highway, and other basic infrastructure improvements. In addition, emigrants' remittances were up, averaging about four billion US dollars per year. It is important to note that the austerity programs of the Central Bloc and the PSD governments well prepared the Portuguese economy for EEC assistance: as the disappointing case of Greece has demonstrated, EEC intervention is not the only ingredient required for economic recovery.

Portugal's membership in the EEC also qualified it to participate in the elections for the European Parliament. Presently comprised of 626 members—of which Portugal has twenty-five—this legislative body's main functions are to approve the EEC's budget, to debate and question decisions of the EEC's Council of Ministers. As of the present time, the European Parliament is not able to initiate legislation, although it appears that it will gain more powers as Europe moves toward greater unification. The PSD managed a plurality in the Portuguese elections for the European Parliament in 1987 and 1989; the PS won a plurality in the 1994 elections.[27]

Table 4.6 Main Macroeconomic Indicators in Portugal, 1988–1990 (as %)

	1988	1989	1990
Private Consumption	+ 6.8	+3.2	+4.5
Public Consumption	+ 5.4	+2.0	+2.2
Exports	+7.2	+16.1	+12.0
Imports	+17.5	+10.6	+13.2
GDP	+4.0	+4.8	+3.9
Inflation	9.6	12.6	13.3
Unemployment	5.6	5.4	5.0
Foreign Debt (US$M)	17,782.0	18,561.0	17,562.0
% of GDP	42.2	37.0	30.0

Source: James Capel European Research, *Update on Portugal* (London: James Capel, 1991), 4.
+Figures cited from Bank of Portugal, *Report on Macroeconomic Indicators*, July 1990.

The 1991 Presidential and Legislative Elections

Four years of economic prosperity and political stability rendered the 1991 electoral cycle anticlimactic.[28] Mário Soares, with the support of the PS and the PSD, was easily reelected on 13 January 1991, with 70 percent of the vote, and in October, Cavaco Silva retained the PSD majority, winning over 50 percent of the votes.

The Presidential Campaign. There were four candidates running for President. For the sake of political stability, and in appreciation of his cooperative relationship with Prime Minister Cavaco Silva, the PSD decided to join the PS and support Mário Soares' reelection bid. The CDS nominated Basílio Horta, who ran a feisty anti-Soares campaign and appealed to conservative PSD voters upset over the party's decision to support Soares. Carlos Carvalhas represented the Communist Party and ran a low-key campaign. He argued that Portugal's economic expansion had left the poor behind, and promised to be attentive to their needs. The UDP and other far-left groups supported Carlos Marques. In the campaign, Marques impressed people as a likable man but did not gain much electoral support. The presidential voting of 13 January 1991 was somewhat overshadowed by the outbreak of the Persian Gulf War.[29] As shown in Table 4.7, Soares was easily reelected.

Table 4.7 Results of the Presidential Election of 13 January 1991

Candidate	% of Vote
Mário Soares	70
Basílio Horta	14
Carlos Carvalhas	13
Carlos Marques	3

Source: Público, 14 January 1991.

The Legislative Campaign. In the fall legislative campaign, Cavaco Silva asked the electorate to allow him to "finish the job." If the PSD did not retain its majority, he threatened to resign as Prime Minister, warning that it was too early to turn the government over to the opposition.[30] The PS, led by Lisbon's mayor, Jorge Sampaío, accused the PSD of overseeing an increase in the national rich-poor divide, and the PCP pointed to the continuing high rates of adult illiteracy in the Alentejo, which reached 40 percent in some areas.[31]

As shown in Table 4.8, the PSD retained a majority in the 6 October 1991 legislative voting. This vote clearly represented a positive assessment of Cavaco's government. The PS maintained its position as the leading opposition party with 29.25 percent, whereas the PCP and the CDS continued to decline, receiving 8.84 percent and 4.39 percent respectively. CDS head Freitas do Amaral resigned after these elections, taking responsibility for the CDS's poor showing.

Table 4.8 Results of the National Assembly Elections of 6 October 1991

Party	CDU	PS	PSN	PSD	CDS
% of Vote	8.84	29.25	1.69	50.43	4.39
Seats Won	17	69	1	130	5

Note: CDU=PCP+MDP+Greens. The PSN (National Solidarity Party) represented the interests of pensioners. The PRD received only 0.61 percent, and has disbanded. The remaining 4.79 percent was divided among smaller parties.
Source: RDP Internacional, Figures of Final Election Results (Lisbon: RDP, 1991).

CONCLUSION

By the end of 1991, there was governmental stability, economic recovery and civilian control over the military. In addition, civil sectors had been voting for the moderate PSD and PS, leaving the PC and CDS at the extremes. Portuguese politics had become so moderate that the leading parties—with the exception of the PCP—ignored the 25 April 1991 commemorations of the 1974 coup.[32] The regime's success at solving problems and meeting expectations since the inauguration of the democratic regime bodes well for its continued existence.

NOTES

1. *Wall Street Journal*, 17 October 1983.

2. *Facts on File World News Digest*, 8 July 1983, 500D1.

3. See an excellent review of the Portuguese economy by Sam Levy, "The Portuguese Economy, 10 Years After," *Wall Street Journal*, 6 June 1984.

4. *Facts on File World News Digest*, 17 June 1983, 444A3.

5. Otelo is quoted in *New York Times*, 21 July 1985.

6. *Diário de Notícias*, 26 November 1984.

7. The prosecution based its case on the testimony of four FP-25 members against Otelo, and on entries in three notebooks seized at his home detailing the organization of a political group known as Global Project. During the trial, the FP-25 continued its activity, attacking the American Embassy twice more. Otelo has since been released on appeal. See *New York Times*, 20 May 1987.

8. *OECD Economic Surveys: Portugal* (Washington, D.C.: Organization for Economic Cooperation and Development, 1986), 1.

9. *Expresso*, 15 June 1985.

10. *Diário de Notícias*, 25 June 1985.

11. See coverage in *Expresso*, 25 May 1985.

12. *Facts on File World News Digest*, 7 February 1986, 84F3.

13. *Expresso*, 14 February 1986.

14. Interview with Vasco Gonçalves, *Expresso*, 14 February 1986.

15. *Expresso*, 22 February 1986.

16. *Facts on File World News Digest*, 1 April 1986, 238F3.

17. *Wall Street Journal*, 18 January 1988.

18. *Facts on File World News Digest*, 1 May 1987, 316G1.

19. *Expresso*, 4 April 1987.

20. Earlier the PS had changed its official rhetoric. Its newly elected President, Vítor Constâncio, influenced delegates at the 1986 Socialist Party congress to make changes in the party's structure, including the deletion of all references to Karl Marx and Marxism in its declaration of principles. See *Facts on File World News Digest*, 11 July 1986, 509C3.

21. See Thomas Gallagher, "Twilight Draws Closer for Portugal's Communists: The General Elections of 19 July 1987," *Journal of Communist Studies* 4, no. 1 (March 1988): 90–95.

22. *Expresso*, 25 July 1987.

23. See editorial by José António Saraiva, "Política à Portuguesa," *Expresso*, 25 July 1987.

24. *Facts on File World News Digest*, 4 September 1987, 648B3.

25. See *Constituição da República Portuguesa* (Lisbon: Porto Editora, 1990), 228–231.

26. *Wall Street Journal*, 24 July 1989. In 1990 the Ford Motor Company announced plans to invest over $2 billion in a new leisure vehicle plant in Setúbal—the largest private investment ever in Portugal. *Público*, 6 July 1990.

27. Matthew Cossolotto, *The 1995 Almanac of European Politics* (Washington, D.C.: Congressional Quarterly, 1995), 221–222.

28. *The Economist: A Survey of Portugal* (London: The Economist, 1988).

29. *Público*, 14 January 1991.

30. *Público* has excellent election coverage.

31. See the special report by Alan Riding, "On Portuguese Farms, a Leftist Dream Withers,"*New York Times*, 17 May 1990.

32. *Público*, 24 April 1991.

5

Summary and Conclusion: The Challenges of Democratic Consolidation in Portugal

This study has examined the challenges of the Portuguese consolidation of democracy. The consolidation involved a multi-faceted dynamic, in which political, military and economic variables interacted. The precise causal relationship among these factors is enigmatic, but it is clear that the overall manner in which the regime's challenges were settled facilitated the process of democratic consolidation. This chapter concludes the argument by summarizing how the new democratic regime in Portugal responded to its political, economic and military challenges from 1976 to 1991.

THE POLITICAL CHALLENGE

The political challenge required that the democratic regime realize governmental stability in Lisbon and develop linkage organizations in civil society. In both of these areas, political parties took center stage.

Realizing Governmental Stability

The question of governmental stability may be subdivided into at least four categories, including the rules of the political game, political learning, ultimate values and how the present regime compares to its predecessors.[1]

Rules of the Game. This dimension of political consensus is central to the process of consolidation: it establishes who the participants will be and how decisions will be reached in the new regime. The Portuguese Constitution of 1976 accords the right to all citizens to participate in the political process and guarantees that the government will respect their civil liberties. These provisions, among others, provide for the operation of a democratic system predicated upon majority rule with assurances that the rights of minorities will also be protected. As such, this system grants "stakes" to even the smallest political formation that seek to offset any tangible benefits associated with extremist anti-system terrorist activities. The rules of the electoral game have facilitated governmental stability as well. The Constitution provides for the use of the d'Hondt system of proportional representation which allocates seats based on the highest average vote obtained in elections. That system has fostered a degree of parliamentary steadiness by limiting the number of parties in the system and by providing incentives for the larger parties to form electoral alliances. Enticing all sides to cooperate within a system of democratic rules, the Constitution has enhanced the durability of the regime.

Political Learning. Political learning by actors in Portugal during the consolidation period should not be underestimated. Prior to 1987 none of the political parties had managed to organize a majority government: there had been five National Assembly elections (forming ten constitutional governments) and three presidential elections (leading to two Presidents, Ramalho Eanes and Mário Soares). The terrorist activities of the FP-25 group also troubled the regime. From 1987 to 1995, however, the political situation was significantly less chaotic as the PSD, under the leadership of Prime Minister Cavaco Silva, held an absolute majority in the National Assembly. Future governments may prefer to rule from a majority coalition, or from a strong minority position, rather than emulate the weak minority Socialist governments of the 1970s.

Ultimate Values. Giovanni Sartori correctly asserts that agreement among political actors regarding the telos of a new regime—although important—is not a necessary condition for the consolidation of a democratic regime.[2] For instance, many conservative political actors objected to the 1976 Constitution's "transition to socialism" clause which obliged Portugal to become a society without classes at an unspecified point in the future. This disagreement between the conservative (i.e. CDS and PSD) and socialist (i.e. PS and PC) political parties over Portugal's ultimate direction did not prevent those conservative political parties from participating in the new democratic system. The principle of electoral legitimacy, which was also incorporated into the Constitution, ultimately enabled those conservative forces—with the somewhat surprising support of the Socialist party—to delete the "transition to socialism" clause democratically in the constitutional revision of 1989. Conversely, the Communist party may someday try to revisit this debate over ultimate values. That is, all of the political actors do not have to share a common vision of the future in order to peacefully compete against one another in the present.

Regime Comparisons. One factor augmenting the stability of the new democratic regime in the late 1970s was that it did not confront a viable alternative political model. As shown in Table 5.1, Thomas Bruneau found in a 1978 survey of Portuguese voters that even though many respondents were less than enamored with the new democratic regime—as evidenced by Mário Soares' low rating—a full 31 percent stated that they did not know which governments governed, or govern, the country best. This raises the issue of "inverse legitimation," which may be defined as "attempts to validate the new regime and even garner support for it by pointing to real or exaggerated faults of the previous one."[3] That is, the "more evil" past regime serves as a reminder that the current regime is at least less of an evil than the previous one. In Portugal, the memory of the long and difficult colonial war, as well as the illegal activities of the PIDE/DGS secret police force, enabled many to accept more readily the slow progress of the new regime. That is not to say that Salazar and Caetano did not have their supporters—35 percent of the respondents ranked their governments as the best—but 65 percent of the respondents preferred governments other than Salazar or Caetano. The poll results reflect a divided and uncertain electorate, who, on the one hand, were not enthralled about their new democratic regime, but, on the other hand, did not seek a return to the previous dictatorship. The lack of a serious alternative political model impeded the rise of a vibrant anti-system party in the 1970s (the efforts of FP-25 notwithstanding) and aided the political stability of the young democratic regime.

Table 5.1 Which Governments or Regimes Governed, or Govern, the Country Best?

Leader	% of Respondents
Salazar	7.
Marcello Caetano	28.
Palma Carlos	1.
Vasco Gonçalves	8.
Pinheiro de Azevedo	3.
Mário Soares (First Constitutional Government)	9.
Don't Know	31.
No Response	13.

Source: Thomas C. Bruneau and Alex Macleod, *Politics in Contemporary Portugal: Parties and the Consolidation of Democracy* (Boulder, CO: Lynne Rienner, 1986), 93.

Extending Stakes to Civil Sectors

Political Parties. The new political parties form a key link between the democratic regime and civil sectors. The Communist Party remains strong in the Alentejo and in the urban areas of Lisbon and Setúbal. The Socialist Party represents a more moderate, centrist element of the electorate, and is influential throughout the country, especially in the central districts. The Social Democrat Party is particularly dominant in the north and in the islands, representing a center-right constituency. The Social Democratic Center Party, while not explicitly religious, is linked to the generally conservative Catholic population in the north and island regions.

Union Organization. After the 25 April 1974 coup, civil sectors were allowed to organize freely and petition the government. At present about 30 percent of the workers are unionized in two major organizations: a Communist-affiliated union, the Confederação Geral dos Trabalhadores Portugueses-Intersindical Nacional (CGTP-IN) and a Socialist union, the União Geral dos Trabalhadores (UGT). Although the unions were quite ideological in the 1970s, especially the CGTP-IN, they have sought more limited and realistic objectives in recent years.

The Roman Catholic Church. Unlike Spain, the Roman Catholic Church has never played an appreciable political role in Portugal. However, Portugal is a Catholic country, and the attitudes of the clergy can impact the regime's overall legitimacy. Since the new democratic political forces have posed no serious threat to religious freedom, the regime has peacefully coexisted with the Church. If the past is instructive, it takes an exceedingly controversial political issue, typically one that threatens the institution itself—such as the radical, anti-clerical politics of the 1974 to 1976 period by some of the MFA officers—to get the Church involved in Portuguese politics.

THE ECONOMIC CHALLENGE

The economic challenge demanded that the constitutional governments provide for stable economic growth and improve the national standard of living. Poor economic conditions limited the ability of the various governments to provide relief for the people from 1976 to 1986. The economic situation has since improved. Political stability after 1987 led to, and benefitted from, economic recovery in the late 1980s and early 1990s.

A Question of Fulfilling Expectations

Undeniably, political and economic successes have reinforced each other during the consolidation of the Portuguese democratic regime. On the one hand, without democratic procedures, government policies would not have enjoyed the legitimacy necessary for implementation in the post-coup era; on the other hand, without sound and successful economic plans, democratic leaders could not have been able to gain and maintain adequate support from civil society for their programs. If the political and economic successes had not reinforced each other, the consolidation of democracy in Portugal might not now seem so promising.

The Working Class. By all objective economic indicators, the Portuguese worker was better off in 1991 than in the mid-1970s. In the first few years of the new democratic regime, however, the economic picture did not look so promising: real wages per capita dropped each year from 1976 to 1984, reaching their lowest point in 1984. The situation has since improved. Under Cavaco Silva's PSD governments, and with EEC support, 250,000 new jobs were added from 1985 to 1990, and unemployment hit the low of 4.7 percent in 1990. The World Bank classified Portugal's economy to be an upper-middle-income, eleventh among the twelve members of the EEC, in 1994.[4] The improved economic standing of the Portuguese worker, combined with the implementation of a political system able to articulate and respond to citizen concerns, has facilitated the consolidation process.

The Business Elite. Traditionally hostile to democracy, the country's leading business groups currently support the new democratic regime. They were swayed by essentially two considerations: the country's traditional European and American political and economic allies supported democratization in Portugal, and the EEC required that Portugal become a fully democratic state before it could approve its membership in the EEC.[5] Notably, EEC membership turned the consolidation of political democracy for the elite into a vehicle for vast economic opportunities and contacts in the richer European countries. Certainly the aggressive pro-capitalist liberalization policies adopted by the government after 1987 facilitated their support for the democratic regime as well. Combined, these factors enabled the business elite to more readily accept the principle of electoral legitimacy.

THE MILITARY CHALLENGE

The military challenge involved whether or not the Council of the Revolution (CR) would accept as legitimate the decisions and policies of the democratically elected representatives, even if they differed with the content of those decisions.

The Principle of Civilian Control Over the Armed Forces

The 1976 Constitution accorded the CR veto power over any legislation it deemed unconstitutional to ensure that the elected governments stay "faithful to the spirit of the Portuguese Revolution of 25 April 1974."[6] That constitutional clause posed an interesting paradox for the young democracy: what would the military do if the people rejected socialism in freely held elections?

All of the speculation came to an end when the CR decided to accept the constitutional revision of 1982 which eliminated the Council of the Revolution. This decision sent the powerful signal to the society that the military establishment was very serious about democratization because it accepted the principle of electoral legitimacy. The election of civilian Mário Soares as President in 1986 was another indication that the military had come to terms with the principle of civilian control in Portugal. Given the fact that MFA officers had proclaimed their military intervention to be a revolution in 1974, this moderate outcome was quite surprising. In this regard Russell Bova has astutely observed that "the radical leaders of the 1974 Portuguese coup were to play midwife to the birth of a liberal democratic order that they had not originally envisioned".[7]

CONCLUSION

It is difficult and perhaps even somewhat arbitrary to pinpoint a precise time at which a country can be said to have completed the consolidation of its democratic regime. In many ways democracy itself is a political process with ongoing phases. However, the positive manner in which the regime's political, economic and military challenges were settled indicates that future politics in Portugal will no longer focus on the comprehensive issues of regime-design (i.e. debates over constitutional revisions), but rather on the more limited details of public policy, typical of legislative debates in established democratic countries.

In a sense, one might say that the process of democratic consolidation in Portugal followed Adam Przeworski's theoretical model in that all of the politically relevant forces (including military, political, business, and labor organizations) eventually subjected their values and interests to the uncertain interplay of democratic institutions. This probabilistic process has involved a delicate process of bargaining and compromise in which all of the key groups in society, including the political elite, the military, business leaders, labor unions and state employees, have participated—enabling the regime to solve its problems and meet rising expectations.[8] Whenever the parties could not resolve their differences, elections were called, and usually set politics in a clear direction. Challenged, pushed, threatened and abused, the new constitutional regime has survived. In the words of Mário Soares, "Portugal now knows what it wants, where it is going, and what it has to do to get there . . . it believes in its capabilities, so often manifest throughout its long history, and knows that it will be able to meet the challenge offered to it."[9]

Given the successful resolution of the political, economic and military challenges in Portugal from 1976 to 1991, it is appropriate to conclude this study with the observation that the Portuguese democratic regime is in very good health, and that the outlook for the continuation of democracy in Portugal is excellent.

NOTES

1. Giovanni Sartori, *Theory of Democracy Reconsidered* (Chatham, NJ: Chatham House Publishers, 1987), 86–171. Also see J. Samuel Valenzuela, "The Challenges of Democratic Consolidation," in Scott Mainwaring, Guillermo O'Donnell and J. Samuel Valenzuela, eds., *Issues in Democratic Consolidation: The New South American Democracies in Comparative Perspective* (Notre Dame: University of Notre Dame Press, 1992), 82–84.

2. Sartori, 86–171.

3. Valenzuela, 78–79.

4. Eric Solsten, ed., *Portugal: A Country Study* (Washington, DC: Library of Congress, 1994), 115–139.

5. See Mário Murteira, *Desenvolvimento, Subdesenvolvimento e o Modelo Português* (Lisbon: Editorial Presença, 1979).

6. See *Constituição da República Portuguesa: As Três Versões Após 25 de Abril 1989/1982/1976* (Lisbon: Porto Editora, 1990), 223.

7. Russell Bova, "Political Dynamics of the Post-Communist Transition: A Comparative Perspective," in Nancy G. Bermeo, ed., *Liberalization and Democratization: Change in the Soviet Union and Eastern Europe* (Baltimore: Johns Hopkins University Press, 1992), 124. The MFA's replacement organization, the Associação 25 de Abril, has not played a particularly important political role, acting more like a social club for old military comrades.

8. See Adam Przeworski, "The Games of Transition," in Mainwaring, O'Donnell and Valenzuela, 105–152. Also see Catherine M. Conaghan, "Capitalists, Technocrats and Politicians: Economic Policy Making and Democracy in the Central Andes," in Mainwaring, O'Donnell and Valenzuela, 229–234.

9. Mário Soares, "Portugal's Democracy," in Kenneth Maxwell and Michael H. Haltzel, *eds., Portugal: Ancient Country, Young Democracy* (Washington, DC: Woodrow Wilson Center Press, 1991), 5; Also see interview with Mário Soares by Vincent Jorge Silva and Teresa de Sousa, *Público* 22–23 March 1992.

References

Aguiar, Joaquim. "The Transition to Democracy in Portugal: The New Political Paradigm and the Role of the Communist Party." Paper delivered to the Friedrich Newmann Foundation, Santiago, Chile, December 1988.

———. "Paradigmas de Decisão Política: Um Modelo de Simulação para Portugal." *Revista de Ciência Política* 3 (Spring 1986): 23–49.

———. *A Ilusão do Poder: Análise do Sistema Partidário Português, 1976–1982*. Lisbon: Dom Quixote, 1982.

Amaral, Diogo Freitas do. "The Constitution and Governance in Portugal." In *The Constitution and the Consolidation of Democracy, 1976–1989*. Edited by Kenneth R. Maxwell and Scott C. Monge. New York: Columbia University, Camões Center, 1991.

Atlas Eleitoral: Resultados Eleitorais, 1975–1980. Lisbon: Editorial Progresso Social e Democracia, 1981.

Baer, B. and A. P. N. Leite. "The Peripheral Economy: Its Performance in Isolation and Integration." *Luso-Brazilian Review* 29 (1992): 18.

Baklanoff, Eric N. "The Political Economy of Portugal's Old Regime: Growth and Change Preceding the 1974 Revolution." *World Development* (August-September 1979): 799–811.

Baldani, Dragisa Popovic. *Eanes: Entre o Ontem e o Amanhã.* Lisbon: Novo Nordica/Tempo Editora, 1986.

Baloyra, Enrique A., ed. *Comparing the New Democracies: Transition and Consolidation in Mediterranean Europe and in the Southern Cone.* Boulder, CO: Westview Press, 1987.

Bandeira, António Rangel. "The Portuguese Armed Forces Movement: Historical Antecedents, Professional Demands and Class Conflict." *Politics and Society* 61 (1976): 1–56.

———. *Military Intervention in Portuguese Politics: Antecedents of the Armed*

Forces Movement. Toronto: Brazilian Studies, 1974.

Barreto, António and Maria Paula Vidal. *Os Partidos Políticos e a Reforma Agrária*. Lisbon: Gabinete de Estudos Rurais, 1980.

Barroso, José Durão. "A Estabilização do Sistema Partidário Português: Alguns Tópicos para uma Discussão." In *In Search of Modern Portugal*. Edited by Eduardo de Sousa Ferreira and Walter C. Opello. Madison: University of Wisconsin Press, 1983.

Bermeo, Nancy Gina. "Democracy in Europe." *Daedalus*, 123 (Spring 1994): 159–178.

———. *Liberalization and Democratization: Change in the Soviet Union and Eastern Europe*. Baltimore: Johns Hopkins University Press, 1992.

———. "Worker Management in Industry: Reconciling Representative Government and Industrial Democracy in a Polarized Society." In *In Search of Modern Portugal*, eds. Lawrence S. Graham and Douglas L. Wheeler. Madison: University of Wisconsin Press, 1983, 181–197.

———. *The Revolution Within the Revolution: Workers' Control in Rural Portugal*. Princeton: Princeton University Press, 1986.

Bogdanowicz-Bindert, Christine A. "Portugal, Turkey and Peru: Three Successful Stabilization Programs Under the Auspices of the IMF." *World Development* 2, no. 1 (1993): 65–70.

Bourdillat, Nicole. "Portugal: Le M.F.A. et l'Institution Militaire dans la Révolution des Oeillets." In *La Politique de Mars: Les Processus Politiques dans les Partis Militaires Contemporains*. Edited by Alain Rouquié. Paris: Le Sycomore, 1981.

Bouscaren, Anthony Trawick. "The Puzzles of Portuguese Politics." *Journal of Social, Political and Economic Studies* 6, no. 3 (1981): 327–344.

Bova, Russell. "Political Dynamics of the Post-Communist Transition: A Comparative Perspective." In *Liberalization and Democratization: Change in the Soviet Union and Eastern Europe*. Edited by Nancy G. Bermeo. Baltimore: Johns Hopkins University Press, 1992.

Brandão de Brito, José Maria. *A Industrialização Portuguesa no Pos-Guerra*. Lisbon: Dom Quixote, 1989.

Bruneau, Thomas C. "Portugal and Democracy: An Unexpected Transition." In *Portugal: Ancient Country, Young Democracy*. Edited by Kenneth Maxwell and Michael Haltzel. Washington, DC: Woodrow Wilson Center Press, 1991.

———. "Political Parties and Democratic Consolidation in Portugal." Paper delivered at the 1990 Annual Meeting of the American Political Science Association, San Francisco, 30 August-2 September 1990.

———. "Discovering Democracy." *The Wilson Quarterly* 9 (1985): 67–81.

———. *Politics and Nationhood: Post-Revolutionary Portugal*. New York: Praeger, 1984.

———. "Continuity and Change in Portuguese Politics: Ten Years After the

Revolution of 25 April 1974." *West European Politics* 7, no. 2 (April 1984): 72–83.

———. "As Dimensões Internacionais da Revolução Portuguesa: Apoios e Constrangimentos no Estabelecimento da Democracia." *Análise Social* 18, no. 72–74 (1982): 72–83.

———. "The Left and the Emergence of Portuguese Liberal Democracy." In *Eurocommunism and Eurosocialism: The Left Confronts Modernity*. Edited by Bernard E. Brown. New York: Cycro, 1979.

Bruneau, Thomas C., and Mário Bacalhau. *Atitudes, Opiniões e Comportamentos Políticos dos Portugueses, 1973–1993*. Lisbon: Fundação Luso Americana Para o Desenvolvimento, 1993.

Bruneau, Thomas C., and Alex Macleod. *Politics in Contemporary Portugal: Parties and the Consolidation of Democracy*. Boulder, CO: Lynne Rienner, 1986.

Cabral, Manuel Villaverde. "Portugal Desde a Revolução." *Análise Social* 23 (Fall 1987): 605–608.

———. *The Portuguese Communist Party: An Interpretation of Fifty Years of History*. Oxford: Saint Anthony's College, 1979.

———. "Sobre o Fascismo e o Seu Advento em Portugal: Ensaio de Interpretação a Pretexto de Alguns Livros Recentes." *Análise Social* 48 (1976): 873–915.

Caetano, Marcelo. *Confidências no Exílio*. Lisbon: Verbo, 1985.

———. *Depoimento*. Rio de Janeiro: Distribuidora Record, 1975.

Caldeira, Reinaldo, and Maria do Ceu Silva, eds. *A Constituição Política da República Portuguesa de 1976*. Amadora: Bertrand, 1976.

Carrilho, Maria. *Forças Armadas e Mudança Política em Portugal no Século XX*. Lisbon: Imprensa Nacional, Casa da Moeda, 1985.

———. "O 25 de Abril e o Papel Político dos Militares—uma Perspectiva Sociológica." *Revista Crítica de Ciências Sociais*, no. 15–17 (May 1985): 77–90.

Carvalho, Otelo Saraiva de. *Alvorada em Abril*. Lisbon: Bertrand, 1977.

———. "Election Program of Otelo Saraiva de Carvalho." *Intercontinental Press* 14 (26 July 1976): 1145–1146.

———. "MFA-do Nascimento à Vitória Final." *Revista Expresso* 27 July 1974: 17–19.

Center for Strategic and International Studies. *Portugal and Spain: Transition Politics*. Washington, DC: Center for Strategic and International Studies, Georgetown University, 1976.

Chilcote, Ronald H. *Transitions from Dictatorship to Democracy*. New York: Taylor and Francis, 1990.

———. *The Portuguese Revolution of 25 April 1974: Annotated Bibliography on the Antecedents and Aftermath*. Coimbra: Centro de Documentação 25 de Abril, Universidade de Coimbra, 1987.

Coelho, Mário Baptista, ed. *Portugal: O Sistema Político e Constitucional, 1974–1987*. Lisbon: Instituto de Ciências Sociais, Universidade de Lisboa, 1989.

Constituição da República Portuguesa: As Três Versões Após 25 de Abril: 1976, 1982, 1989. Lisbon: Porto Editora, 1989.

Corkill, David. "The Political System and the Consolidation of Democracy in Portugal." *Parliamentary Affairs* (October 1993): 517–532.

Cossolotto, Matthew. *The 1995 Almanac of European Politics*. Washington, DC: Congressional Quarterly, 1995.

Costa, Carlos, ed. *As Eleições no Portugal de Abril*. Lisbon: Edições Avante, 1980.

Costa, Eduardo Freitas da. *Spínola: O Anti-Geral*. Lisbon: Fernando Pereira, 1979.

Costa-Pinto, António. *Salazar's Dictatorship and European Fascism: Problems and Perspectives of Interpretation*. New York: Columbia University Press, 1995.

———. "The Radical Right in Contemporary Portugal." In *The Far Right in Western and Eastern Europe*. Edited by Luciano Cheles, Ronnie Ferguson and Michalina Vaughan. New York: Longman, 1995.

———. *Os Camisas Azuis: Ideologia, Elites e Movimentos Fascistas em Portugal, 1914–1945*. Lisbon: Estampa, 1994.

Courakis, Anthony S., Fátima Moura-Roque, and George Tridimas. "Public Expenditures and Growth in Greece and Portugal: Wagner's Law and Beyond." *Applied Economics* 25 (1993): 125–134.

Cruz, Manuel Braga da, and Miguel Lobo Antunes. "Revolutionary Transition and the Problems of Parliamentary Institutionalization: The Case of the Portuguese National Assembly." In *Parliament and Democratic Consolidation in Southern Europe*. Edited by Ulrike Liebert and Maurizio Cotto. London: Pinter, 1990.

Cunha, Carlos. *The Portuguese Communist Party's Strategy for Power, 1921–1986* (New York: Garland, 1993).

Cunhal, Álvaro. "Results and Prospects of the Portuguese Revolution." *World Marxist Review* 20 (January 1977): 18–31.

———. *Portugal: The Democratic and National Revolution*. New York: International Publishers, 1975.

———. *Discursos Políticos*. Lisbon: Edições Avante!, 1974.

———. *Portugal: L'Aube de la Liberté*. Paris: Notre Temps/Monde, 1974.

———. *A Revolução Portuguesa*. Lisbon: Dom Quixote, 1972.

Dahl, Robert. *Democracy and Its Critics*. New Haven: Yale University Press, 1989.

———. *Polyarchy*. New Haven: Yale University Press, 1971.

———. *A Preface to Democratic Theory*. Chicago: University of Chicago Press, 1956.

Diamond, Larry. "Crisis, Choice and Structure: Reconciling Alternative Models for Explaining Democratic Success and Failure in the Third World." Paper delivered at 1989 Annual Meeting of the American Political Science Association, Atlanta, 31 August-3 September 1989.

Diamond, Larry, Juan J. Linz and Seymour Martin Lipset, eds. *Democracy in Developing Countries.* 4 vols. Boulder: Lynne Rienner Publishers, 1989.

DiPalma, Giuseppe. *To Craft Democracies: An Essay on Democratic Transitions.* Berkeley: University of California Press, 1991.

Diário de Notícias. *Palavras no Tempo.* Lisbon: Diário de Notícias Editoria, 1991.

Domingos, Emídio da Veiga. *Portugal Político: Análise das Instituições.* Lisbon: Rolim, 1977.

Domínguez, Jorge, and Samuel P. Huntington. "Political Development." In *Handbook of Political Science.* Edited by Fred I. Greenstein and Nelson W. Polsby. Reading, MA: Addison Wesley, 1975.

Downs, Charles R. *Revolution at the Grassroots: Community Organizations in the Portuguese Revolution.* New York: SUNY Press, 1989.

Eleições em Abril: Diário de Campanha. Lisbon: Libir Editions, 1975.

Esping-Anderson, Gosta. "Budgets and Democracy: Towards a Welfare State in Spain and Portugal, 1960–1986." In *Developing Democracy.* Edited by Ian Budge and David McKay. Beverly Hills: Sage 1994.

Ethier, Diane. *Democratic Transition and Consolidation in Southern Europe, Latin America and Southeast Asia.* London: Macmillan, 1990.

European Free Trade Association. *The Effects of EFTA on the Economics of Member States.* Geneva: EFTA, 1969.

Faye, Jean Pierre, ed. *O Portugal de Otelo: A Revolução no Labirinto.* Lisbon: Socicultur, 1977.

Ferreira, Eduardo de Sousa, and Walter C. Opello, eds. *Conflict and Change in Portugal, 1974–1984.* Lisbon: Teorema, 1985.

Ferreira, F. A. Gonçalves, ed. *15 Anos da História Recente de Portugal, 1970–1984.* Lisbon: Antonio Dias, 1985.

Ferreira, Hugo Gil, and Michael Marshall. *Portugal's Revolution, Ten Years On.* Cambridge: Cambridge University Press, 1986.

Ferreira, José Medeiros. *Portugal em Transe.* Aveiro: Pandora, 1985.

———. "Os Militares e o Regime Democrático–o MFA: uma Intervenção Singular." In *Semanário: 25 de Abril: 10 Anos Depois.* Lisbon: Associação 25 de Abril Fundação Calouste Gulbenkian, 1984.

Figueiredo, Antonio de. *Portugal: Fifty Years of Dictatorship.* Harmondsworth: Penguin, 1975.

França, Luis de. *Comportamento Religioso da População Portuguesa.* Lisbon: Morães Editores, 1981.

Gallagher, Thomas. "Twilight Draws Closer for Portugal's Communists: The

General Elections of 19 July 1987." *Journal of Communist Studies* 4, no. 1 (March 1988): 90–95.

———. "Democracy in Portugal Since the 1974 Revolution." In *Conflict and Change in Portugal, 1974–1984*. Edited by Eduardo de Sousa Ferreira and Walter C. Opello. Lisbon: Teorema, 1985.

———. *Portugal: A Twentieth Century Interpretation*. Manchester: Manchester University Press, 1983.

———. "Portugal's Bid for Democracy: The Role of the Socialist Party." *West European Politics* 2 (May 1979): 198–217.

Gaspar, Carlos. "Constitutional Politics and Regime Stability." In *Portugal: The Constitution and the Consolidation of Democracy, 1976–1989*. Edited by Kenneth R. Maxwell and Scott C. Monje. New York: Camões Center, Columbia Center, 1991.

———. "Portuguese Communism Since 1976: Limited Decline." *Problems of Communism* 39 (January-February) 1990: 45–63.

Gaspar, Jorge. "10 Anos de Democracia: Reflexos na Geofaphia Política." In *Conflict and Change in Portugal, 1974–1984*. Edited by Eduardo de Sousa Ferreira and Walter C. Opello. Lisbon: Teorema, 1985.

———. *Portugal em Mapas e em Números*. Lisbon: Livros Horizonte, 1981.

Georgel, Jacques. *O Salazarismo*. Lisbon: Dom Quixote, 1985.

Goldey, David B. "Elections and the Consolidation of Portuguese Democracy, 1974–1983." *Electoral Studies* 2 (1983): 229-240.

Gonçalves, Vasco. *Discursos, Conferências de Imprensa, Entrevistas*. Lisbon: Seara Nova, 1977.

González, Juan Carlos Hernández. "La Crisis de Legitimidad Política y el Proceso de Recuperación Democrática en Portugal (1978–1980)." *Revista de Politica Comparada* (Madrid) 8 (1982): 95–128.

Gracio, Sergio Miguel. "Portugal: Cinco Anos Depois de Abril." In *Temas de Ciências Humanas*. Edited by Marco Aurelio Nogueira. São Paulo: Livraria Editora Ciências Humanas, 1979.

Graham, Lawrence S. *The Portuguese Military and the State: Rethinking Transitions in Europe and Latin America*. Boulder, CO: Westview Press, 1993.

———."Bureaucratic Politics and the Problem of Reform in the State Apparatus." In *In Search of Modern Portugal*. Edited by Lawrence S. Graham and Douglas L. Wheeler. Madison: University of Wisconsin Press, 1983.

———. "O Estado Português Visto à Partir de Baixo." *Análise Social*, no. 72–74 (1982): 959–975.

———. "The Military in Politics: The Politicization of the Portuguese Armed Forces." In *Contemporary Portugal: The Revolution and Its Antecedents*. Edited by Lawrence S. Graham and Harry M. Makler. Austin: University of Texas Press, 1979.

———. *Portugal: The Decline and Collapse of an Authoritarian Order*. Beverly Hills, CA: Sage, 1975.

———. "The Parliament in Portuguese Constitutional History." *Iberian Studies* 7 (Spring 1978): 22–29.

Graham, Lawrence S., and Harry M. Makler, eds. *Contemporary Portugal: The Revolution and Its Antecedents*. Austin: University of Texas Press, 1979.

Graham, Lawrence S., and Douglas L. Wheeler, eds. *In Search of Modern Portugal*. Madison: University of Wisconsin Press, 1983.

Grayson, George. "Portugal and the Armed Forces Movement." *Orbis* 19 (Summer 1975): 335–378.

———. "Portugal and the Future." *Current History* 68 (March 1975): 19–113.

Hammond, John L. *Building Popular Power: Workers' and Neighborhood Movements in the Portuguese Revolution*. New York: Monthly Review Press, 1988.

———."The Armed Forces Movement and the Portuguese Revolution." *Journal of Political and Military Sociology* (Spring 1982): 71–101.

———."Electoral Behavior and Political Militancy." In *Contemporary Portugal: The Revolution and Its Antecedents*. Edited by Lawrence S. Graham and Harry M. Makler. Austin: University of Texas Press, 1979.

Harsgor, Michael. *The Washington Papers: Portugal in Revolution*. Beverly Hills, CA: Sage, 1976.

Harvey, Robert. "Portugal: Democracy's Balance-Sheet." *The World Today* (January 1979): 24–38.

———. *Portugal: Birth of a Democracy*. London: Macmillan, 1978.

Herr, Richard, ed. *The New Portugal: Democracy and Europe*. Berkeley: University of California Press, 1992

Holland, Stuart. "Dependent Development: Portugal as a Periphery." In *Underdeveloped Europe: Studies in Core-Periphery Relations*. Edited by Dudley Seers, Bernard Schaffer and Marja Liisa Kiljunen. London: Harvester Press, 1979.

Huntington, Samuel P. *The Third Wave: Democratization in the Late Twentieth Century*. Norman: University of Oklahoma Press, 1991.

———. "Will More Countries Become Democratic?" In *Global Dilemmas*. Edited by Samuel P. Huntington and Joseph S. Nye. Cambridge, MA: Harvard University Press, 1985.

———. *Political Order in Changing Societies*. New Haven: Yale University Press, 1968.

Insight Team of the *London Sunday Times*. *Insight on Portugal*. London: Andre Deutsch, 1975.

Joxe, Alain. "Le Mouvement des Forces Armées Portugaises." *Politique Etrangère* (Paris) 6 (1974): 659–688.

Karl, Terry Lynn and Phillipe C. Schmitter. "The Conceptual Travels of Transitologists and Consolidologists: How Far to the East Should They Attempt to Go? *Slavic Review*, 53 (Spring 1994): 173–185.

———. "Modes of Transition in Latin America, Southern and Eastern Europe." *International Social Science Journal* 128 (May 1991): 269–284.

———. "What Democracy Is . . . and Is Not." *Journal of Democracy*, 2 (Summer 1991): 75–89.

Kayman, Martin. *Revolution and Counterrevolution in Portugal*. London: Merlin Press, 1987.

Kramer, Jane. "Letter from Lisbon." *The New Yorker* (23 September 1974): 101–104.

Levine, Daniel H. "Paradigm Lost: Dependence to Democracy." *World Politics*, 2 (April 1988): 377–394.

Lewis, J. R. and Allan M. Williams. "Social Cleavages and Electoral Performance: The Social Basis of Portuguese Parties, 1976–1983." *West European Politics* 7, no. 2 (April 1984): 119–137.

Liebert, Ulrike, and Maurizio Cotto, eds. *Parliament and Democratic Consolidation in Southern Europe*. London: Pinter, 1990.

Lijphart, Arendt. *Democracies*. New Haven: Yale University Press, 1984.

———. *Democracies in Plural Societies*. New Haven: Yale University Press, 1977.

Linz, Juan J. "Spain and Portugal: Critical Choices." In *Western Europe: The Trials of Partnerships*. Edited by David S. Lander. Lexington, MA: Lexington Books, 1977.

———. "Totalitarian and Authoritarian Systems." In *Handbook of Social Science*, 3. Edited by Fred Greenstein and Nelson Polsby. Reading, MA: Addison Wesley, 1975.

Linz, Juan J. and Alfred Stepan. "Political Crafting of Democratic Consolidation or Destruction: European and South American Comparisons." In *Democracy in the Americas: Stopping the Pendulum*. Edited by Robert Pastor. New York: Holmes and Meier, 1989.

———, eds. *The Breakdown of Democratic Regimes*. 4 vols. Baltimore: Johns Hopkins University Press, 1978.

López-Pintor, Rafael. "Mass and Elite Perspectives in the Process of Transitions to Democracy." In *Comparing the New Democracies: Transition and Consolidation in Mediterranean Europe and in the Southern Cone*. Edited by Enrique A. Baloyra. Boulder, CO: Westview Press, 1987.

Macedo, Jorge Braga de. "*A Constituição e a Economia: Como Superar o Bloqueio.*" Paper delivered at the Conference "The Constitution and the Consolidation of Democracy in Portugal, 1976–1989," Camões Center, Columbia University, 10 November 1989.

Macedo, Jorge Braga de, and Simon Serfaty, eds. *Portugal Since the Revolution: Economic and Political Perspectives*. Boulder, CO:

Westview Press, 1981.

Maier, Phil. *Portugal: The Impossible Revolution*. New York: Free Life Editions, 1977.

Mainwaring, Scott, Guillermo O'Donnell and J. Samuel Valenzuela, eds. *Issues in Democratic Consolidation: The New South American Democracies in Comparative Perspective*. Notre Dame, IN: University of Notre Dame Press, 1992.

Manuel, Paul C. "The Challenges of Democratic Consolidation in Portugal." Paper delivered to the Iberian Studies Group, Center for European Studies, Harvard University, 26 February 1996.

———. "Portuguese Foreign Policy Since 1976: A Case of Elite Bargaining?" Paper delivered to the 1995 Annual Meeting of the American Political Science Association, Chicago, 2 September 1995.

———. *Uncertain Outcome: The Politics of the Portuguese Transition to Democracy*. Lanham, MD: University Press of America, 1995.

———. "The Process of Democratic Consolidation in Portugal." Paper delivered to the Department of Portuguese and Brazilian Studies, Brown University, 3 November 1994.

———. "Whence Portuguese Democracy?" Paper delivered to the IV Meeting of the International Conference Group on Modern Portugal, University of New Hampshire, 24 September 1989.

Maravall, José María, Luiz Pereira and Adam Prezorski, eds. *Economic Reforms in New Democracies*. Cambridge: Cambridge University Press, 1993.

Marcadé, Jacques. *Le Portugal au XX Siècle, 1910–1985*. Paris: Presses Universitaires de France, 1988.

Marques, A. H. de Oliveira. *A History of Portugal*. New York: Columbia University Press, 1976.

Maxwell, Kenneth. *The Making of Portuguese Democracy*. New York: Cambridge University Press, 1995.

———. *Portugal in the 1980s: Dilemmas of Democratic Consolidation*. Westport, CT: Greenwood Press, 1986.

———. *"Regime Overthrow and the Prospects for Democratic Transition in Portugal." In Transitions from Authoritarian Rule: Southern Europe*. Edited by Guillermo O'Donnell, Phillipe C. Schmitter and Lawrence Whitehead. Baltimore: Johns Hopkins University Press, 1986.

———. *Portugal: Ten Years After the Revolution*. New York: Research Institute on International Change, Columbia University, 1984.

———. *The Press and the Rebirth of Iberian Democracy*. Westport, CT: Greenwood Press, 1983.

———. *The Transition in Portugal*. Washington: Woodrow Wilson Center, 1982.

———. "The Communists and the Portuguese Revolution." *Dissent* 27 (Spring 1980): 194–206.

———. "The Thorns of the Portuguese Revolution." *Foreign Affairs* 54 (January 1976): 250–270.

———. "Portugal Under Pressure." *New York Review of Books* 22 (29 May 1975): 20–30.

———. "Portugal: A Neat Revolution." *New York Review of Books* 21 (17 April 1975): 29–35.

Miranda, Jorge. *O Essencial Sobre a Constituição Portuguesa*. Lisbon: Casa da Moeda, 1986.

Morrison, Rodney J. *Portugal: Revolutionary Change in an Open Economy*. Boston: Auburn House, 1981.

Mujal–León, Eusébio. "The Portuguese Elections of 1983: The Portuguese Party System in Flux." Unpublished Manuscript, 1984.

———. "Communism and Revolution in Portugal." In *Eurocommunism and Détente*. Edited by Rudolf L. Tokes. New York: Council of Foreign Relations, New York University Press, 1978.

———."The PCP and the Portuguese Revolution." *Problems of Communism* 26 (January-February 1977): 21–41.

Murteira, Mário. *A Política Económica numa Sociedade em Transição*. Lisbon: Presenca, 1983.

———. *Desenvolvimento, Subdesenvolvimento e o Modelo Português*. Lisbon: Presença, 1979.

———."O Modelo Português de Subdesenvolvimento." *Economia e Socialismo* 19 (October 1977): 3–13.

———. *Portugal na Década de 60: Industrialização e Emigração*. Lisbon: Presença, 1974.

Nataf, Daniel. *Democratization and Social Settlements: The Politics of Change in Contemporary Portugal*. Albany, NY: SUNY Press, 1995.

Nataf, Daniel and Elizabeth Sammis. "Classes, Hegemony and Portuguese Democratization." In *Transitions from Dictatorship to Democracy*. New York: Taylor and Francis, 1990.

O'Donnell, Guillermo. "On the State, Democratization and Some Conceptual Problems." *World Development* 21 (1993): 1355–1369.

O'Donnell, Guillermo, Philippe C. Schmitter and Lawrence Whitehead, eds. *Transitions from Authoritarian Rule: Southern Europe*. 4 vols. Baltimore: Johns Hopkins University Press, 1986.

Oliveira, César. "Transição de Consolidação da Democracia em Portugal." *Pensamiento Iberoamericano: Revista de Económica Política* (Madrid) 14 (July-December 1988): 299.

O'Neil, Brian Juan. *Social Inequality in a Portuguese Hamlet: Land, Late Marriage and Bastardy, 1870–1978*. Cambridge: Cambridge University Press, 1984.

Opello, Walter C. *Portugal: From Monarchy to Pluralist Democracy*. Boulder: CO: Westview Press, 1991.

———. Portugal's Parliament: An Organizational Analysis of Legislative Performance." *Legislative Studies Quarterly* 11 (August 1986): 291–319.

———. *Portugal's Political Development*. Boulder, CO: Westview Press, 1985.

———. "Portugal's Administrative Elite: Social Origins, and Political Attitudes." *West European Politics* 6 (January 1983): 63–74.

———. "Actividades, Papeis e Orientações Ideológicas de Sociais-Democratas Portugueses: Estudo de uma Amostra." *Análise Social 18, no.* 72–74 (April-December 1982): 947–958.

———. "Portugal." In *Political Parties of Europe*. Edited by Vincent C. McHale. Westport, CT: Greenwood Press, 1981.

———. "The New Parliament in Portugal." *Legislative Studies Quarterly* 3 (May 1978): 309–334.

———. "The Parliament in Portuguese Constitutional History." *Iberian Studies* 7 (Spring 1978): 22–29.

———. "The Second Portuguese Republic: Politico-Administrative Decentralization Since 25 April 1974." *Iberian Studies* 7 (Autumn 1978): 43–48.

Opello, Walter C. and William Claggett. "The Dynamics of West European Party Systems: The Portuguese Case." *Polity* 17 (Fall 1984): 165–178.

Organization for Economic Cooperation and Development. *OECD Economic Surveys: Portugal*. Washington, DC: OECD July 1986.

Pasquino, Gianfranco. "Party Elites and Democratic Consolidation: Cross-National Comparisons of Southern European Experience." In *Securing Democracy: Political Parties and Democratic Consolidation in Southern Europe*. Edited by Geoffrey Pridham. New York: Routledge, 1990.

Payne, Stanley G. "Dictatorship and Democratization in Southern Europe: A Historian's Perspective." *Modern Greek Studies Yearbook* 4 (1988): 1–13.

———. *Fascism*. Madison: University of Wisconsin Press, 1980.

———. *A History of Spain and Portugal*. 2 vols. Madison: University of Wisconsin Press, 1973.

Pimlott, Ben. "Socialism in Portugal: Was It a Revolution?" *Government and Opposition* 12 (Summer 1977): 332–350.

Pintado, Miguel Rodrigues and Alvaro Mendonça. *Os Novos Grúpos Económicos*. Lisbon: Texto Editora, 1989.

Porch, Douglas. *The Portuguese Armed Forces and the Revolution*. Stanford: Hoover Institute Press, 1977.

Poulantzas, Nicos. *The Crisis of the Dictatorships: Portugal, Greece and Spain*. London: New Left Press, 1976.

Pridham, Geoffrey. *Encouraging Democracy: The International Context of Regime Transition in Southern Europe*. New York: St. Martin's Press,

1991.

———. *Securing Democracy: Political Parties and Democratic Consolidation in Southern Europe*. London: Routledge Press, 1990.

———. *The New Mediterranean Democracies: Regime Transition in Spain, Greece and Portugal*. London: Frank Cass, 1984.

———. "Party Government in the New Iberian Democracies." *The World Today* 40 (January 1984): 12–21.

Pridham, Geoffrey, Eric Herring and George Sanford, eds. *Building Democracy: The International Dimension of Democratization in Eastern Europe*. New York: St. Martin's Press, 1994.

Przeworski, Adam. "The Games of Transition." In *Issues in Democratic Consolidation: The New South American Democracies in Comparative Perspective*. Edited by Scott Mainwaring, Guillermo O'Donnell and J. Samuel Valenzuela. Notre Dame, IN: University of Notre Dame Press, 1992.

———. *Democracy and the Market*. Cambridge: Cambridge University Press, 1991.

———. "Some Problems in the Study of the Transition to Democracy." In *Transitions from Authoritarian Rule: Comparative Perspectives*. Edited by Guillermo O'Donnell, Philippe C. Schmitter and Lawrence Whitehead. Baltimore: Johns Hopkins University Press, 1986.

Putnam, Robert. *Making Democracy Work: Civic Traditions in Modern Italy*. Princeton: Princeton University Press, 1993.

Raby, D.L. *Fascism and Resistance in Portugal*. Manchester: University of Manchester, 1988.

Robinson, Richard A. L. *Contemporary Portugal: A History*. London: Allen and Unwin, 1979.

Rueschemeyer, Dietrich, Evelyne Huber Stephens and John D. Stephens. *Capitalist Development and Democracy*. Chicago: University of Chicago Press, 1993.

Rustow, Dankwart. "Transitions to Democracy: Toward a Dynamic Model." *Comparative Politics* 2 (April 1970): 337–363.

Sá Carneiro, Francisco. *Francisco Sá Carneiro, Textos*. 6 vols. Lisbon: Editorial Progresso Social e Democracia, 1990.

———. *O Ideário Político de Francisco Sá Carneiro*. Edited by José Augusto Seabra. Lisbon: Comissão Recordar Sá Carneiro no 10 Aniversário da Sua Morte, 1990.

———. *Impasse*. Lisbon: Macroplan, 1978.

———. *Por uma Social-Democracia Portuguesa*. Lisbon: Dom Quixote, 1975.

Salazar, Antonio de Oliveira. *Discursos e Notas Políticas*. Coimbra: Centelha, 1976.

Santos, Boaventura de Sousa. *O Estado e a Sociedade em Portugal, 1974–1984*. Lisbon: Biblioteca das Ciências do Homen, Edições

Afrontamento, 1990.

———. "A Crise e a Reconstituição do Estado em Portugal, 1974–1984." *Revista Crítica de Ciências Sociais* 14 (November 1984): 7–29.

———. "Law and Revolution in Portugal: The Experience of Popular Justice After the 25th of April 1974." In *The Politics of Informal Justice*. Edited by Richard L. Abel. New York: Academic Press, 1982.

Saraiva, José António. "Política à Portuguesa" in *Expresso*, 25 July 1987.

———. "As Forças Armadas e o Poder Político." *Revista Comerativa do 25 de Abril* (April 1980): 3–5.

Saraiva, José Hermano. *História Concisa de Portugal*. Mem Martins: Europa-América, 1987.

———. *O 25 de Abril Visto da História*. Amadora: Bertrand, 1976.

Sartori, Giovanni. *The Theory of Democracy Reconsidered*. Chatham, NJ: Chatham House Publishers, 1987.

———. *Democratic Theory*. Westport, CT: Greenwood Press, 1973.

Schmidt, Hans O. *Economic Stabilization and Growth in Portugal*. Washington, DC: International Monetary Fund, 1981.

Schmitter, Philippe C. "Speculations About the Prospective Demise of Authoritarian Regimes and Its Possible Consequences." *Revista de Ciência Política* 1 (1985): 83–102, and 2 (1985): 125–144.

———. "Liberation by Golpe" *Armed Forces and Society* 2 (November 1975): 5–33.

———. *Corporatism and Public Policy in Authoritarian Portugal*. Beverly Hills, CA: Sage, 1975.

Schumpeter, Joseph A. *Capitalism, Socialism and Democracy*. New York: Harper Torchbooks, 1962.

Schwartzman, Kathleen. *The Social Origins of Democratic Collapse: The First Portuguese Republic in the Global Economy*. Lawrence: University of Kansas Press, 1989.

Sérgio, António. *Brève Interpretação da História de Portugal*. Lisbon: Sá da Costa, 1978.

Slavitt, David R. *Salazar Blinks*. New York: Atheneum, 1988.

Smelser, Neil, ed. *On Society and Social Change*. Chicago: Univerity of Chicago Press, 1973.

Soares, Dulce M. "Social Concertation and the Democratic Social Consensus: Theory and Praxis in the Portugal of the 1980s." Paper delivered to the Iberian Studies Group, Center for European Studies, Harvard University, 17 March 1995.

Soares, Mário. *Intervenções*. 11 vols. Lisbon: National Press, 1993.

———."Portugal: Accomplishments and Goals," in *Portugal: Ancient Country, Young Democracy*. Edited by Kenneth Maxwell and Michael Haltzel. Washington DC: Woodrow Wilson Press, 1990.

Solsten, Eric ed., *Portugal: A Country Study*. Washington, D.C.: Library of

Congress, 1994.

Spínola, António de. *País sem Rúmo: Contribúto para a História de uma Revolução*. Lisbon: Scrire, 1978.

———. *Ao Serviço de Portugal*. Lisbon: Bertrand, 1976.

———. *Portugal e o Futuro*. Lisbon: Arcadia, 1974.

Stobel, Lester. *Portuguese Revolution 1974–1976*. New York: Facts on File, 1976.

Stepan, Alfred. *Rethinking Military Politics*. Princeton: Princeton University Press, 1988.

———. "State Power and the Strength of Civil Society in the Southern Cone of Latin America." In *Bringing the State Back In*. Edited by Peter B. Evans, Dietrich Rueschmeyer and Theda Skocpol. New York: Cambridge University Press, 1985.

———. *The Military in Politics*. Princeton: Princeton University Press, 1971.

Stepan, Alfred, and Cindy Skach. "Constitutional Frameworks and Democratic Consolidation: Parliamentarianism versus Presidentialism." *World Politics* 46 (October 1993): 1–22.

U.S. Senate, Committee on Foreign Relations. *Portugal and Spain in Search of New Directions: A Report by Senator Claiborne Pell*. Washington, DC: U.S. Government Printing Office, 1976.

———. *Portugal in Transition: A Report by Senator Mike Mansfield*. Washington, DC: U.S. Government Printing Office, 1976.

Valenzuela, Arturo. *The Breakdown of Democratic Regimes: Chile*. Baltimore: Johns Hopkins University Press, 1978.

Valenzuela, Arturo, and J. Samuel Valenzuela. "Modernization and Dependency." *Comparative Politics* (July 1978): 535–557.

Valenzuela, J. Samuel. "Democratic Consolidation in Post–Transitional Settings: Notion, Process, and Facilitating Conditions." In *Issues in Democratic Consolidation: The New South American Democracies in Comparative Perspective*. Edited by Scott Mainwaring, Guillermo O'Donnell and J. Samuel Valenzuela. Notre Dame, IN: University of Notre Dame Press, 1992.

———. "Labor Movements in Transitions to Democracy: A Framework for Analysis." *Comparative Politics* 21, no. 4 (July 1989): 445–472.

Vitorino, António. "The Politics of Constitutional Revision." In *Portugal: The Constitution and the Consolidation of Democracy, 1976–1989*. Edited by Kenneth R. Maxwell and Scott C. Monje. New York: Camões Center, Columbia University, 1991.

Wheeler, Douglas L. "The Honor of the Army." In *The Search for Modern Portugal: The Revolution and Its Antecedents*. Edited by Lawrence S. Graham and Henry M. Makler. Austin: University of Texas Press, 1983.

———. *Republican Portugal: A Political History, 1910–1926*. Madison:

University of Wisconsin Press, 1978.

Wiarda, Howard. *The Transition to Democracy in Spain and Portugal.* Washington, DC: American Enterprise Institute, 1989.

———. *Corporatism and Development: The Portuguese Experience*. Amherst: University of Massachusetts Press, 1977.

World Bank. *Portugal: Current and Prospective Economic Trends*. Washington: The World Bank, 1978.

Zenha, Salgado. *Por uma Política de Concórdia e Grandeza Nacional.* Lisbon: Editoria Perspectivas e Realidades, 1976.

Index

About the Author

PAUL CHRISTOPHER MANUEL is Assistant Professor and Chair in the Department of Politics at St. Anselm College in New Hampshire. He holds degrees from Georgetown University and Boston University.

ISBN 0-275-94849-8

90000>

EAN

9 780275 948498

HARDCOVER BAR CODE